CHAMORRO
WORD BOOK

Marilyn C. Salas
Edited by Josefina Barcinas
Illustrated by Roland Miranda

BESS
PRESS

3565 Harding Ave. Honolulu, Hawai'i 96816 • (808) 734-7159 • Fax (808) 732-3627 • www. besspress.com

Library of Congress Cataloging-in-Publication Data

Salas, Marilyn C.
    Chamorro word book / Marilyn C.
Salas ; edited by Josefina Barcinas ;
illustrations by Roland Miranda.
        p.   cm.
    Includes illustrations, glossary.
    ISBN 1-57306-192-1
    1. Chamorro language -
Dictionaries - English.   I. Barcinas,
Josefina, ed.   II. Miranda, Roland,
ill.
PL5295.4.S24 1998   499.21-dc20

Certified by:

Mary Ann S. Taijito
Ge'helo'

Table of Contents

Foreword

"Chamorro" is the name of the people and the language. Although the precise origin of the people is unknown, most historical researchers agree that the Chamorros have their origin in Southeast Asia.

The Chamorro language belongs to the Austronesian language family. The Austronesian languages include all the traditional languages of Indonesia, Melanesia, Micronesia, the Philippines, and Polynesia, except Papuan, Negrito languages, and the languages of the Australian aborigines.

Chamorro is a distinct language with dialects of central Guam, southern Guam, Saipan, Rota, and Tinian. It has been in print for three hundred years and has undergone numerous changes in the pronunciation system as a result of the Spanish, American, German, and Japanese administrations of the Mariana Islands and studies of the language.

This book contains the official orthography adopted and accepted by the Kumision i Fino' Chamorro (Chamorro Language Commission).

The *Chamorro Word Book* celebrates language and culture through pictures and special words. It contains the most widely used basic words to assist the beginning Chamorro speaker.

In presenta este na lepblo para i uson-miyu. (We present this book for your use.) It was written with love, harmony and care for the preservation of the Chamorro language and culture of future generations and for those who have an interest in learning Chamorro.

The author of the *Chamorro Word Book*, Marilyn C. Salas, received her B.A. and M.Ed. degrees from the University of Guam (UOG). She received her Ph.D. in Reading at the University of Arizona. As an assistant professor and the director of the Multicultural Education and Resource Center (MERC), University of Guam, she is involved in various activities centered on culture and education. Marilyn is the editor of various Micronesian Child Books and the author of *Lepblo Para Tåne' Famagu'on I Isla: A Chamorro/English Interactive Book for Island Children.*

The editor, Josefina Barcinas, is a member of the Kumision I Fino' Chamoru (Chamorro Language Commission). She is widely known for her active participation in the development of Chamorro materials for language education. Josefina holds a master's degree in Elementary Education/Administration and Supervision. She teaches Chamorro 101 at UOG.

The illustrator, Roland Miranda, has been a freelance graphic designer and artist since 1973. Born and raised on Guam, Roland has illustrated several books and is presently an editorial cartoonist for the *Pacific Daily News.* He has several Best Editorial Cartoon Awards from the Guam Press Club and is also a recipient of the Governor's Art Awards. Roland is a member of the Acha'ot Guahan Siha and the Communications Artist Guild of Guam (CAGG).

Pronunciation Guide

The Chamorro language uses the alphabetic system. There are twenty-four letters in the Chamorro alphabet: eighteen consonants and six vowels. Most Chamorro consonants are pronounced like their English equivalents. There are some exceptions:

ch = ts — like ca<u>ts</u>: che'lu

ñ=nya— like o<u>ni</u>on: ñamu

ng — like ki<u>ng</u>: nganga'

y = ds — like su<u>ds</u>: yunga'

k (unaspirated) — like s<u>k</u>ate: kånnai

p (unaspirated) — like s<u>p</u>eak: pugua

t (unaspirated) — like s<u>t</u>and: toktok

The six vowels in the Chamorro language are i, u, e, o, a, and å.

WHEN UNSTRESSED IN OPEN SYLLABLES

i — like ee in s<u>ee</u>: låhi

u — like u in stat<u>u</u>e: hågu

WHEN UNSTRESSED IN CLOSED SYLLABLES

e — like i in s<u>i</u>t: låpes

o — like u in p<u>u</u>t: gupot

a — like a in f<u>a</u>t: at<u>a</u>n

å — like a in f<u>a</u>ther: månu

' = glottal stop

How to Use This Word Book

Hafa Adai! Welcome to the world of Chamorro words, words that can teach and encourage learning. This word book is not simply a dictionary or an alphabetized list of words. Through the use of illustrations, it shows you what words "look" like—what they mean in everyday life. There are words about food that will make you hungry; words about family members and activities you will recognize; words about celebrations that will make you want to dance.

Each reader has personal reasons for opening this book, and each reader will find different ways to enjoy it: Chamorro adults might use it to prepare their youngsters for reading. A language teacher might use it to help English speakers learn Chamorro or Chamorro speakers learn English. This word book can also be a valuable resource about Chamorro culture.

First-Language Development

Reading preparation: Adults and children reading together

Research tells us that children whose first-language speaking skills are well developed can learn to read more easily than children who fall behind in this area. But before children can speak fluently, they must develop good listening skills, and this word book provides abundant opportunities for both listening and speaking. Stories almost leap from the pages. Listening, telling, and retelling them can develop a child's understanding of a language. Using the words and illustrations on page five as examples, here are some ways storytelling can help youngsters connect speech to print:

Open the book with your child and describe the pictures you see. If a picture reminds you of an experience, talk about it. If it reminds you of a legend, tell it. Let your child listen to your voice and your words.

Build a story. Guide with questions that lead to the words on the page. Help your child begin to understand the connection between spoken and printed words. The dialogue below is an example of how you and your child can talk about the pictures.

Adult: Look at this picture! These people are part of a family. Who do you think this lady is?

Child: The grandmother.

Adult: Yes, she is. These words (point to "nanan biha") mean "grandmother." She's bringing some food to the man in the chair. Who do you think he is?

Child: The grandfather.

Adult: Of course. (Point to the word and picture.)
Now, let's use our imaginations. What have grandmother and grandfather been doing? Why is grandfather hungry? What kind of food do you think grandmother has prepared? What do you think they will do after eating?

When you have built your story around the picture, ask the child to retell it to you. Let your child speak. When one of the words on the page is mentioned, point to it. Don't interrupt the flow of speech; just show the child that you are listening. By pointing to the words as they are used, you illustrate that the spoken word can also be written.

Second-Language Learning

Chamorro for English Speakers
English for Chamorro Speakers

At the University of Guam, more people than ever before—people from a variety of ethnic backgrounds—are enrolling in Chamorro classes. Many Chamorro who have grown up in English-speaking communities are now interested in regaining their Chamorro language abilities. Teachers of Chamorro are interested in sharpening their language skills. Others want to improve their English-speaking abilities. This word book can be helpful for teaching and learning either language, and it can be used in similar ways for both languages. It is important for learners to not only hear a new language but also practice it, and therefore, the key activities are listening, telling, and retelling stories.

As a language teacher, you can use the storytelling and story-building techniques described above as pre-literacy activities. However, some changes in approach are recommended for classroom use. For example, stories should be simplified to make them understandable to most students. Also, students should be prepared for the stories they hear. If you introduce new vocabulary and provide time for practice, students will become familiar with new words and will understand them when they hear them again. Finally, you can correct students by using examples as they practice the language. As the teacher, you are the language authority, and students expect your guidance.

The following, using page five as an example, is a sample lesson using the word book. The lesson is designed for beginners and has four parts: picture description, student restatement of the description, student vocabulary practice, and storytelling.

TEACHER'S TALK	STUDENT'S TALK	PURPOSE
Picture description "Look at this picture. These two people are at home. Grandmother is giving some food to Grandfather."	(repetition optional) You may want students to repeat your sentences as a way to start getting their tongues used to the language.	To introduce vocabulary in sentences using simple grammar.
Student restatement "What can you tell me about the picture?" "Yes, Grandmother is giving food to Grandfather. Do you visit your grandmother? Does she give you food?"	"Grandmother giving food." (example)	To give students practice using the vocabulary. To correct the student by modeling the correct form. Also, to repeat and expand the presentation of the vocabulary.
Vocabulary practice "Ask each other about the picture." Demonstrate with one student so the other students understand what you want them to do.	(quizzing each other) "Who's this?"	To review vocabulary and practice question forms.
Storytelling Now you're ready to tell a story to students. Use a lot of repetition; make use of the pictures often; and even act things out to help the students understand.		To develop listening comprehension of connected language.

During the first lesson, the students are mainly listeners. As they comprehend and become more fluent, you can increase their speaking roles by encouraging them to describe, restate, practice, and tell stories. The same lesson is applicable whether you are teaching Chamorro or English.

Chamorro Cultural Awareness and Appreciation

Because the words are arranged by topic and are clearly illustrated, the word book presents a wealth of information about Chamorro culture. By looking at the pictures, an individual, parent and child, or teacher and class can explore the cultural similarities and differences they notice. The following is an example of how a teacher might lead a class while using the word book to increase students' understanding and appreciation of Chamorro culture and of cultural diversity in general.

For this example, look at the picture on page 13: It shows a young man paying respect to an elderly man. Before students look at the picture, have them draw pictures showing how a young person can show respect to an older person. When they share their pictures with each other, they should note similarities and differences and make a list of common characteristics they find in their drawings. Then have the students look at the picture in the word book. In small groups or as a whole class, discuss the similarities and differences between students' perceptions of respectful behavior and the word book pictorial description of the Chamorro custom. The discussion will inevitably go in many directions!

Conclusion

The word book has something for everyone, and the suggestions in this section are by no means the only ways to use the book. We're presenting these ideas here because the areas of *first-language development, second-language learning*, and *cultural awareness and appreciation* are certainly important ones. Hopefully the reader will find these suggestions helpful, and the word book an enjoyable and useful resource.

Timothy Donahue
Pacific Resources for Education and Learning

saludu yan di'åriu na sinangan siha
greetings and daily expressions

saludu yan di'åriu na sinangan siha

greetings and daily expressions

Buenas dihas.
Good morning.

Buenas tåtdes.
Good afternoon.

Buenas noches.
Good evening.

Håfa adai!
Hello!

Håfa tatatmanu håo?
How are you?

Maolek ha' yu'.
I'm just fine.

Håyi na'ån-mu?
What is your name?

I na'ån-hu si _____.
My name is _____.

Despensa yu'
put fabot.
Please excuse me / I'm sorry.

Maila' hålom.
Come in.

Si Yu'os ma'åse'.
Thank you.

Mångge i _____?
Where is the _____?

Mångge i kemmon?
Where is the restroom?

Esta ora.
It's time.

Ki ora?
What time is it?

Tåya' guaha.
It doesn't matter.

Maolek ha'.
It's all right.

Tåotåo månu håo?
Where are you from?

Ginen manu hao?
Where did you come from?

Para amånu-håo?
Where are you going?

Kåo malago' hao
gumimen?
Would you like to drink?

saludu yan di'åriu na sinangan siha
greetings and daily expressions

Kåo siña hu ayuda
håo?
May I help you?

Yanggen ti un lalålo',
kåo siña un ayuda yu'?
*If you don´t mind, can you
help me?*

Hu gof agradesi i
inayuda-mu.
I really appreciate your help.

Hunggan.
Yes.

Åhe'.
No.

Ñålang yu'.
I´m hungry.

Må'ho yu'.
I´m thirsty.

Hu guaiya håo.
I love you.

Adios.
Goodbye.

Adios esta agupa'.
Goodbye until tomorrow.

Adios estaki manali'e'
hit ta'lo.
Goodbye until we meet again.

Ta a'ali'e' despues.
See you later.

familia

family

nånan biha	tåta	subrinu
tåtan bihu	påtgon låhi	kiñåda
nåna	påtgon pålao'an	kiñådu
neni	tihu	primu
tiha	subrina	primu

familia *family*

nånan biha
grandmother

tåtan bihu
grandfather

familia *family*

nåna
mother

neni
baby

familia *family*

tiha *auntie*

familia _family_

tåta _father_

påtgon låhi
son

påtgon
pålao'an
daughter

familia *family*

tihu *uncle*

subrinu *nephew*

subrina *niece*

familia *family*

kiñåda *sister-in-law*

kiñådu
brother-in-law

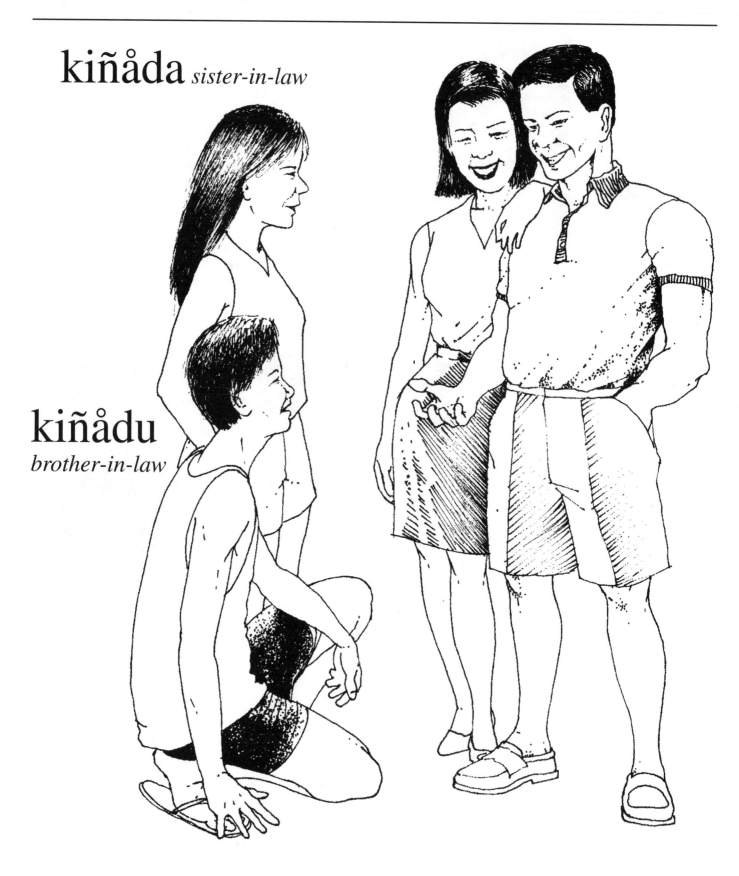

familia *family*

prima *female cousin*   primu *male cousin*

espesi'åt na palåbra siha

special words

respetu	mandaña	klåsi
mannginge'	ina'fa'maolek	inagofli'e'
ñot	adahi	konsederasion
ñora	inadahi	ika
ina'guaiya	ina'påtte	chinchule'
ina'ayuda	agradesi	
ayuda	amåpble	

espesi'åt na palåbra siha *special words*

mannginge'
kiss or smell hand

ñot
respect to elderly man

respetu
respect

espesi'åt na pålabra siha *special words*

respetu
respect

mannginge'
kiss or smell hand

ñora
respect to elderly woman

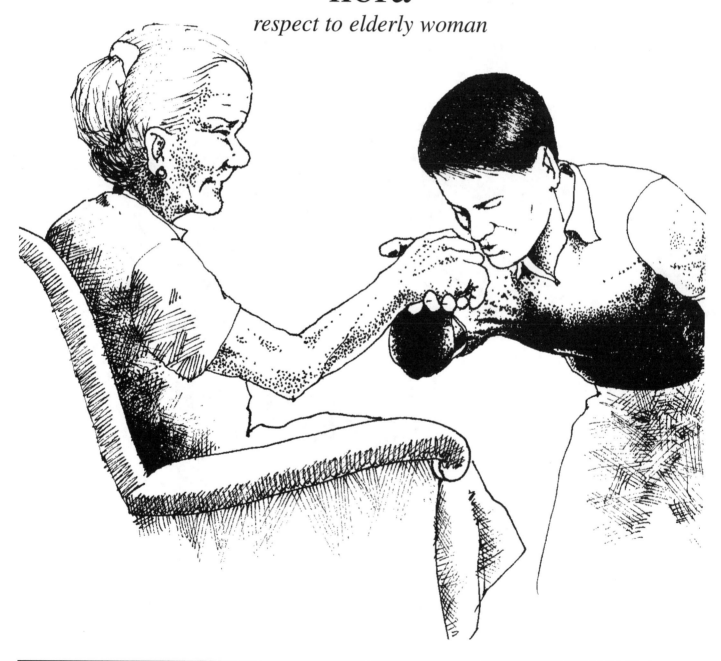

espesi'åt na palåbra siha *special words*

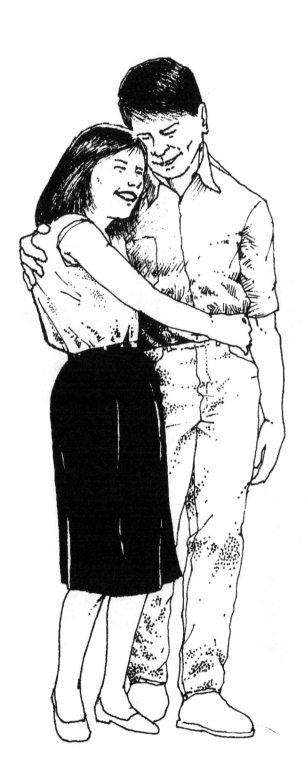

ina'guaiya
love

espesi'åt na palåbra siha *special words*

ina'ayuda (noun)   ayuda (verb)
help

mandanña
getting together

ina'fa'maolek
getting along

adahi/inadahi
care

espesi'åt na palabra siha *special words*

ina'påtte
share

agradesi
appreciate

amåpble/klåsi
kind

inagofli'e'
kindness

konsederasion
consideration

espesi'åt na palåbra siha *special words*

ika
gift-giving (sad occasions)

chinchule'
gift-giving (happy occasions)

isla
island

åtdao	påkyo	unai
somnak	tåsi	tåhgong
trongkon niyok	kanton tåsi	atungo
niyok	haggan	tingteng
månglo'	guihan	(pened-
uchan	saddok	dong hånom)

isla *island*

åtdao
sun

somnak
sunshine

niyok
coconut

trongkon niyok
coconut tree

månglo'
breeze or wind

uchan
rain

påkyo
typhoon

isla _island_

tåsi
ocean

kanton tåsi
shore

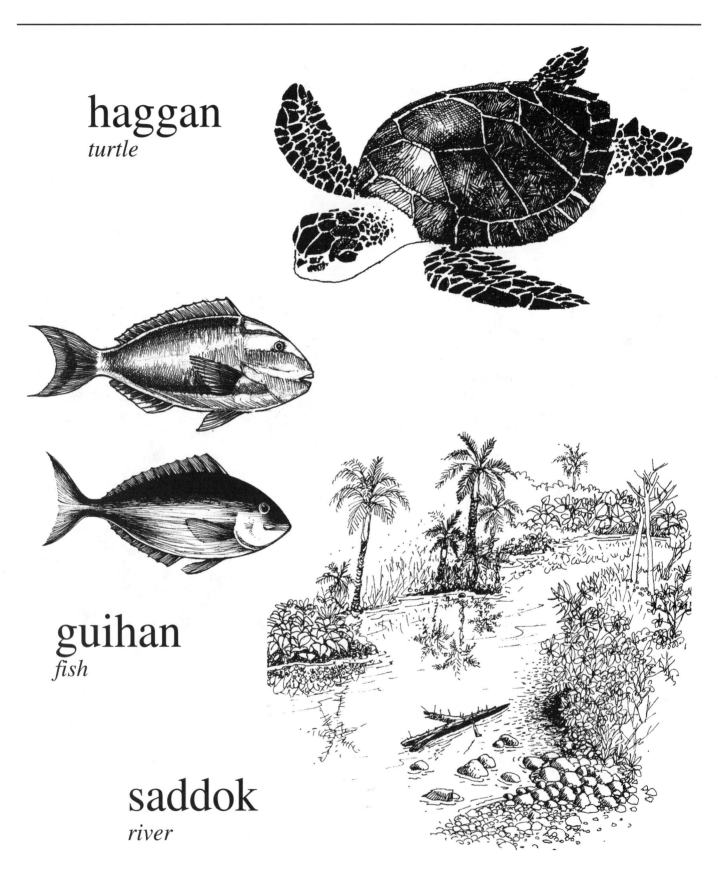

haggan
turtle

guihan
fish

saddok
river

isla *island*

unai
sand

atungo'
friends

tåhgong
shell

tingteng (peneddong hånom)
waterfall

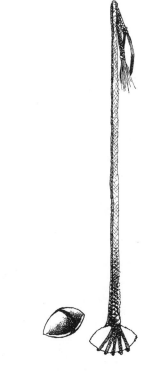

tradision/
kostumbre
tradition

lommok	åmot	haguet
lusong	påsu	tokcha'
mitåti	kusinan	åcho' atupat
månu	sanhiyong	atupat
mestisa	hotno	latte
suruhånu	plomu	

tradision/kostumbre *tradition*

lommok
pestle

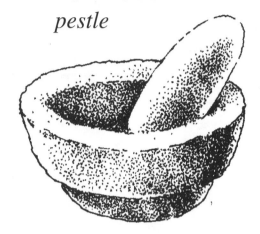

lusong
grinding bowl (mortar)

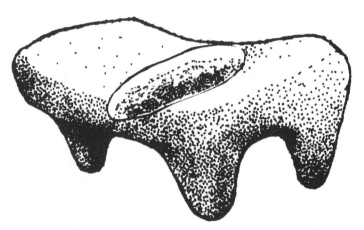

mitåti
corn grinding stone

månu
pestle

mestisa
attire

tradision/kostumbre *tradition*

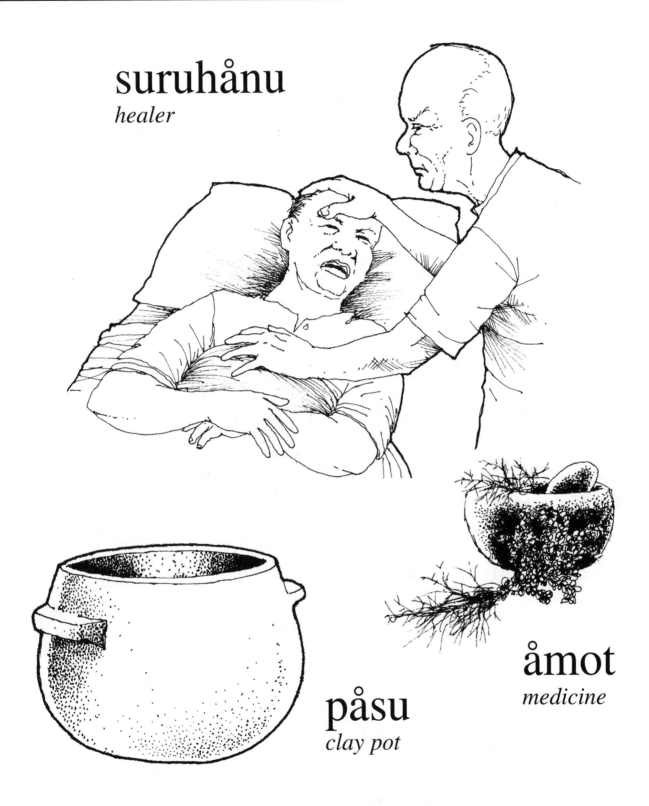

suruhånu
healer

påsu
clay pot

åmot
medicine

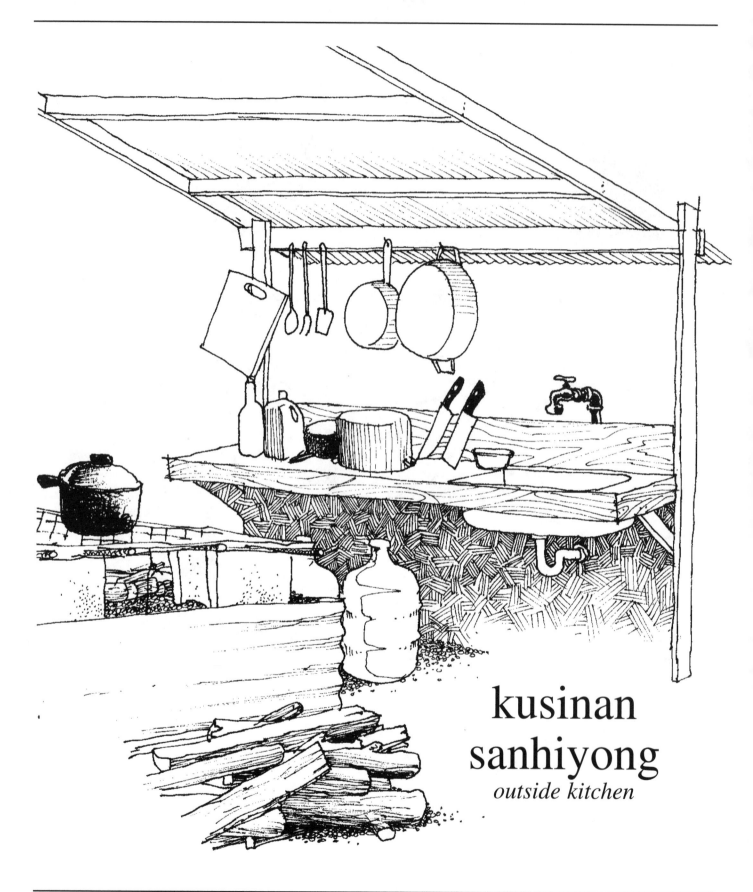

kusinan sanhiyong
outside kitchen

tradision/kostumbre *tradition*

hotno
oven

latte
stone pillar for building

plomu
sinker

atupat
sling

åcho'
atupat
slingstone

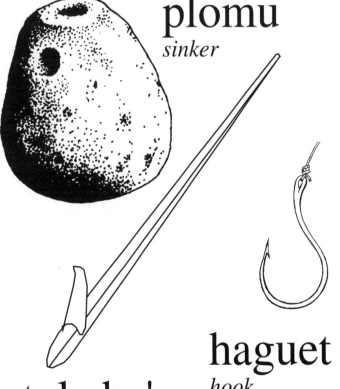

tokcha'
fishing spear

haguet
hook

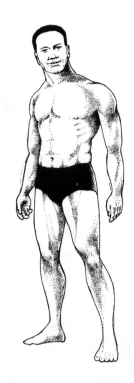

tåtaotao

body

ulu	ulu	fåsu
tongho/kueyu	måta	talanga
apåga	hå'i	gapotulu
pecho	sehas	kånnai
tuyan	åttadok	kålulot
tåtalo'	gui'eng	dåma'gas
tommon kånnai	påchot	muñekan kånnai
trongkon kånnai	nifen	åddeng
tommo	låbios	kålulot åddeng
petna	åchai	dedeggo

tåtaotao *body*

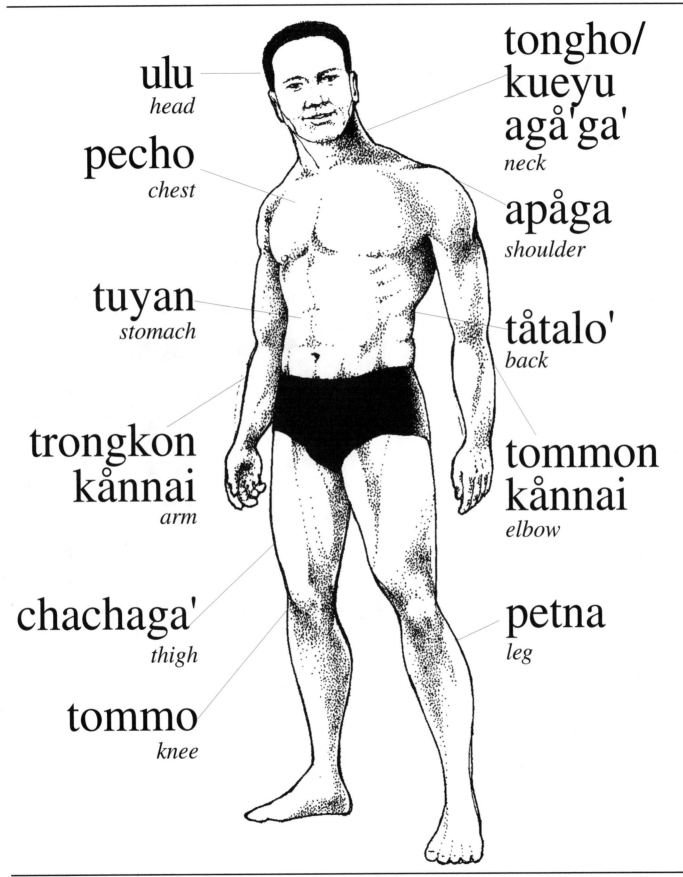

ulu
head

pecho
chest

tuyan
stomach

trongkon
kånnai
arm

chachaga'
thigh

tommo
knee

tongho/
kueyu
agå'ga'
neck

apåga
shoulder

tåtalo'
back

tommon
kånnai
elbow

petna
leg

tåtaotao *body*

ulu
head

måta
face

hå'i
forehead

sehas
eyebrow

åttadok
eye

gui'eng
nose

påchot
mouth

nifen
teeth

låbios
lips

åchai
chin

fåsu
cheek

gapotulu
hair

talanga
ear

tåtaotao *body*

kånnai
hand

kålulot
finger

dåma'gas
thumb

muñekan kånnai
wrist

åddeng
foot

kålulot åddeng
toe

bayogu
ankle

dedeggo
heel

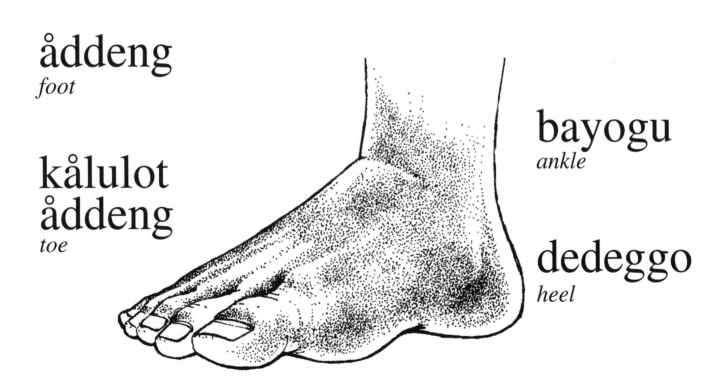

i lamasan gupot
the fiesta table

saosao kånnai	kelaguen månnok	kafe
plåtu	kåddon månnok	bilembines
tenidot	chalakiles	kåhet
kuchåla	åhu	melon
pån	ensalådan batåtas	papåya
titiyas	hågon suni	alageta
hineksa'	ensalådan golla	mångga
fina'denne'	atulen ilotes	piña
lemmai	buñelos aga'	åtes
chotda (green)	hinetnon babui	laguanå
aga'(ripe)	kalamai	anonas
dågon håya	kek Chamoru	åbas
tininon kostiyas	apigige'	chandiha
hammon	brohas	pupulu
uhang	chå	pugua'
pånglao	hånom	
månnok	chigo' fruta	

i lamasan gupot
the fiesta table

saosåo
kånnai
napkin

plåtu *plate*

tenidot
fork

pån
bread

hineksa'
rice

fina'denne'
hot sauce

titiyas
tortillas

i lamasan gupot
the fiesta table

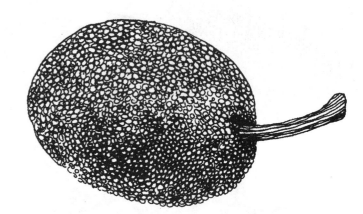

suni *taro*

chotda
banana (green)

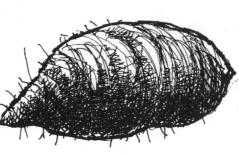

lemmai
breadfruit

dågon håya
yam

aga'
banana (ripe)

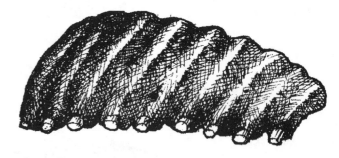

tininon kostiyas
barbecued spareribs

i lamasan gupot

the fiesta table

hammon
ham

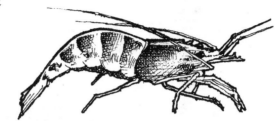

uhang
shrimp

pånglao
crab

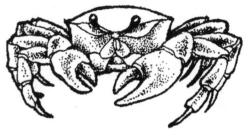

månnok
chicken

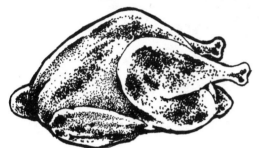

kelaguen månnok
lemon chicken

kåddon månnok
chicken soup

chalakiles
rice porridge

åhu
young coconut dessert

i lamasan gupot
the fiesta table

ensalådan batåtas
potato salad

hagon suni
taro leaf

ensalådan gollai
vegetable salad

atulen ilotes
corn soup

buñelos aga'
banana doughnuts

i lamasan gupot
the fiesta table

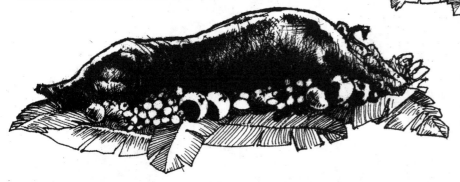

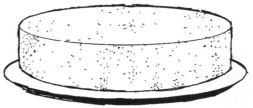

hinetnon babui
roast pig

kalamai
corn pudding

kek Chamoru
Chamorro cake

apigige'
*young coconut
(grilled)
with starch*

brohas
sponge cake

chå
tea

hånom
water

chigo' fruta
fruit juice

kafe *coffee*

i lamasan gupot
the fiesta table

bilembines
star apple

kåhet
orange

melon
melon

papåya
papaya

piña
pineapple

mångga *mango*

alageta' *avocado*

i lamasan gupot
the fiesta table

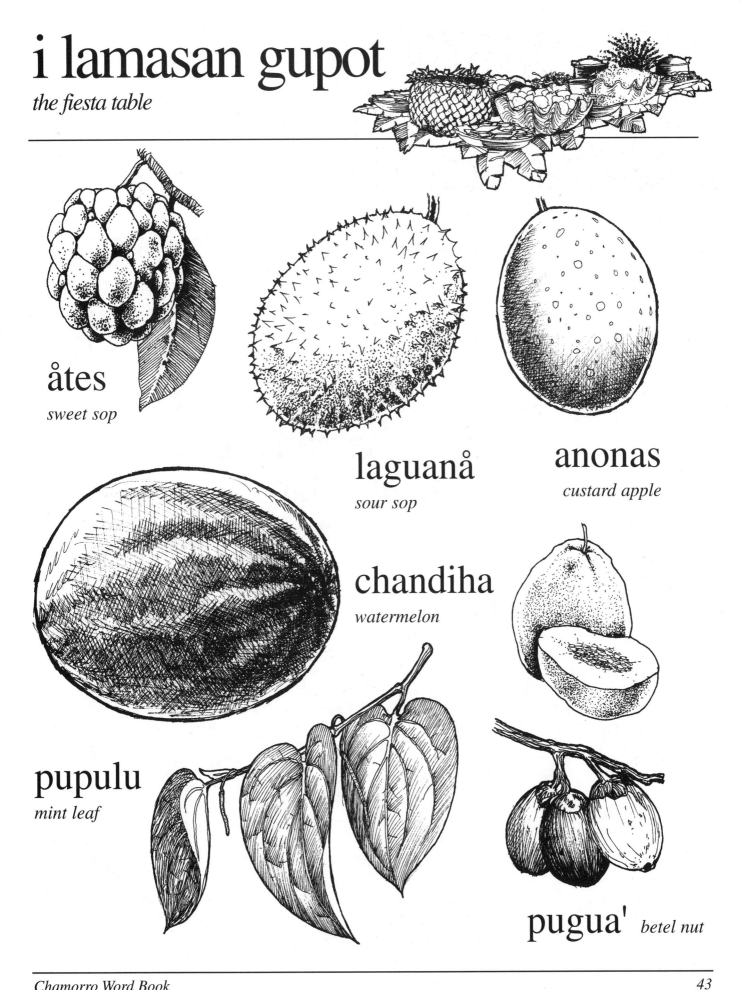

åtes
sweet sop

laguanå
sour sop

anonas
custard apple

chandiha
watermelon

pupulu
mint leaf

pugua' *betel nut*

figura, minnedong, yan tinahlang
shapes, sizes, and weight

lokka'	onsa	estreyas
dikike'	libra	diamånte
midiånu	tunilåda	triånggolo
makkat	dalalai/	rektånggolo
ñalalang	masoksok	adamelong
kadada'	yommok	mediu sitkolo
dångkolo	aridondo	
anåkko'	kuadrao	

figura, minnedong, yan tinahlang
shapes, sizes and weight

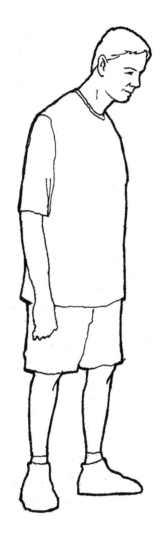

lokka'
tall

dikike'
small

midiånu
medium

figura, minnedong, yan tinahlang
shapes, sizes and weight

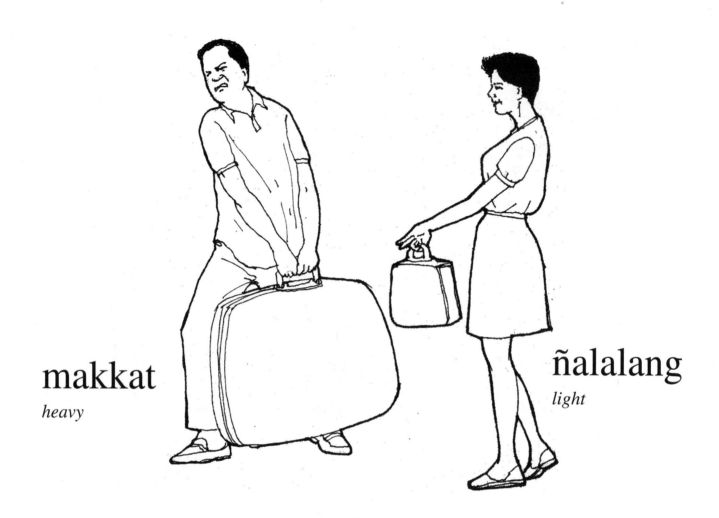

makkat
heavy

ñalalang
light

Other words

kadada' *short*

dångkolo *large*

anåkko' *long*

onsa *ounce*

libra *pound*

tunilåda *ton*

figura, minnedong, yan tinahlang
shapes, sizes and weight

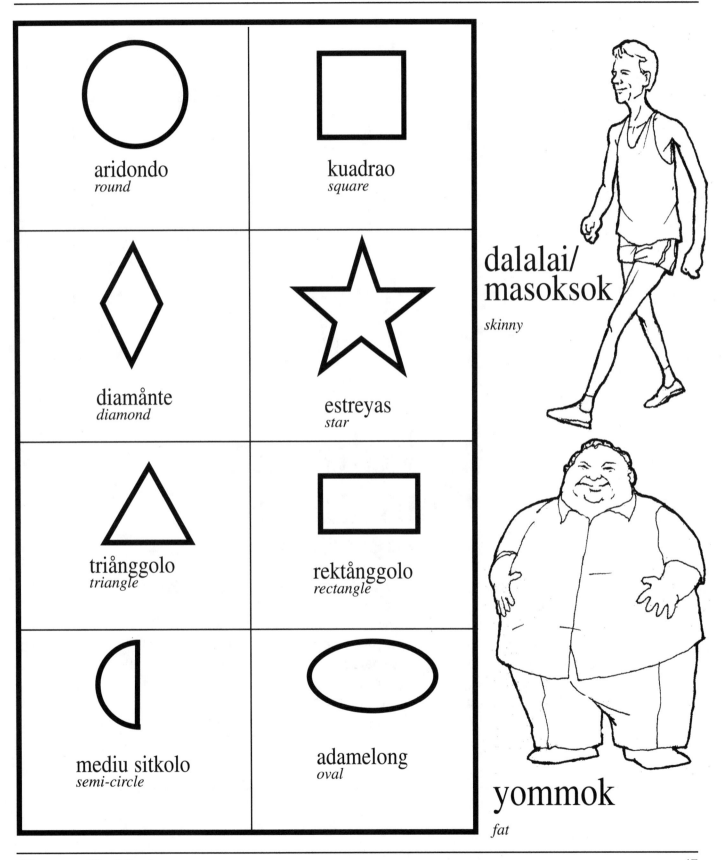

aridondo
round

kuadrao
square

diamånte
diamond

estreyas
star

triånggolo
triangle

rektånggolo
rectangle

mediu sitkolo
semi-circle

adamelong
oval

dalalai/
masoksok

skinny

yommok
fat

attikulu para manma usa
things to wear

magågu	changkletas/yore'	magågon maigo'
chinina	sandalihas	tuhong
franela	meyas	sentoron
bestidu	sapåtos goma	tråhen numangu
lupes	sapåtos	katsunes umo'mak
katsunes	påñu	mestisa
katsunes kadada'	magågon bahåki	

attikulu para manma usa
things to wear

magågu
clothes

chinina
shirt

franela
t-shirt

bestidu
dress

katsunes kadada'
shorts

katsunes
pants

lupes *skirt*

attikulu para manma usa
things to wear

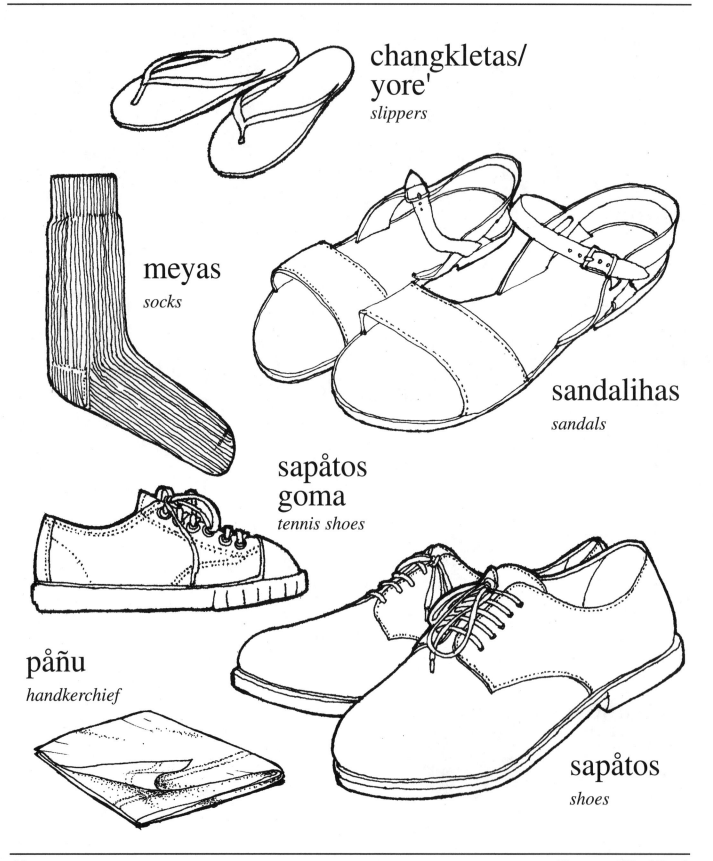

changkletas/
yore'
slippers

meyas
socks

sandalihas
sandals

sapåtos
goma
tennis shoes

påñu
handkerchief

sapåtos
shoes

attikulu para manma usa
things to wear

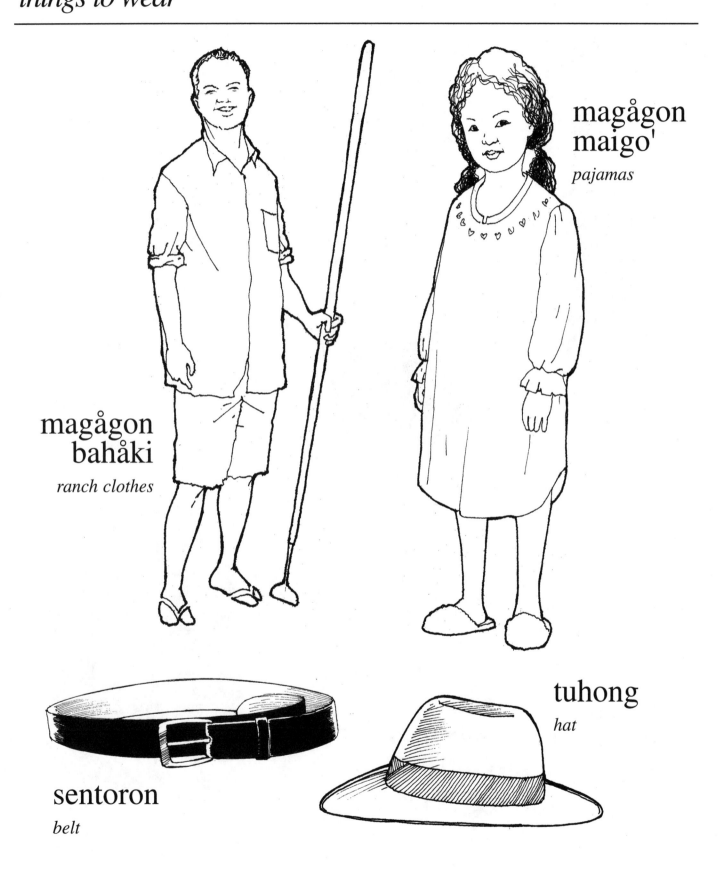

magågon maigo'

pajamas

magågon bahåki

ranch clothes

tuhong

hat

sentoron

belt

attikulu para manma usa
things to wear

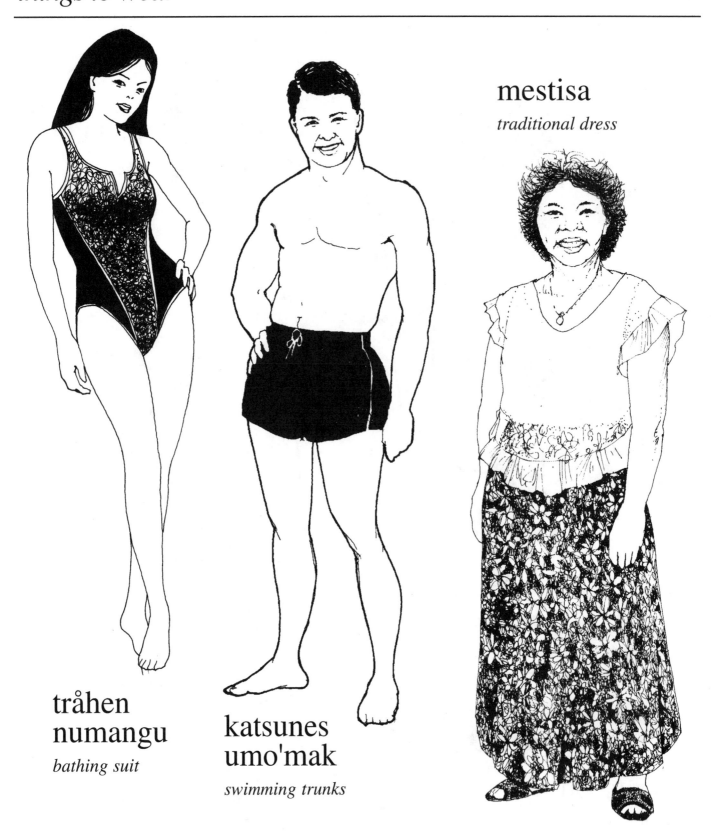

mestisa
traditional dress

**tråhen
numangu**
bathing suit

**katsunes
umo'mak**
swimming trunks

silibrasion familia
family gatherings

gupot i sengsong
Ha'ånen Sånta
  Marian Kåmalen
Åñu Nuebu
Simåna Sånta
Påsgua

Ha'ånen Mannåna
Ha'ånen Mantåta
baotismo
konfetmasion
komple'åños
entieru

Ha'ånen Mannå'i
  Gråsia
Noche Buena
umakamo'
gradu'asion

silibrasion familia *family gatherings*

gupot i sengsong
village fiesta

Ha'ånen Sånta Marian Kåmalen
Our Lady of Camarin Day

Åñu Nuebu
New Year

Simåna Sånta
Holy Week

Påsgua
Easter

Ha'ånen Mannåna
Mother's Day

Ha'ånen Mantåta
Father's Day

silibrasion familia *family gatherings*

baotismo
christening

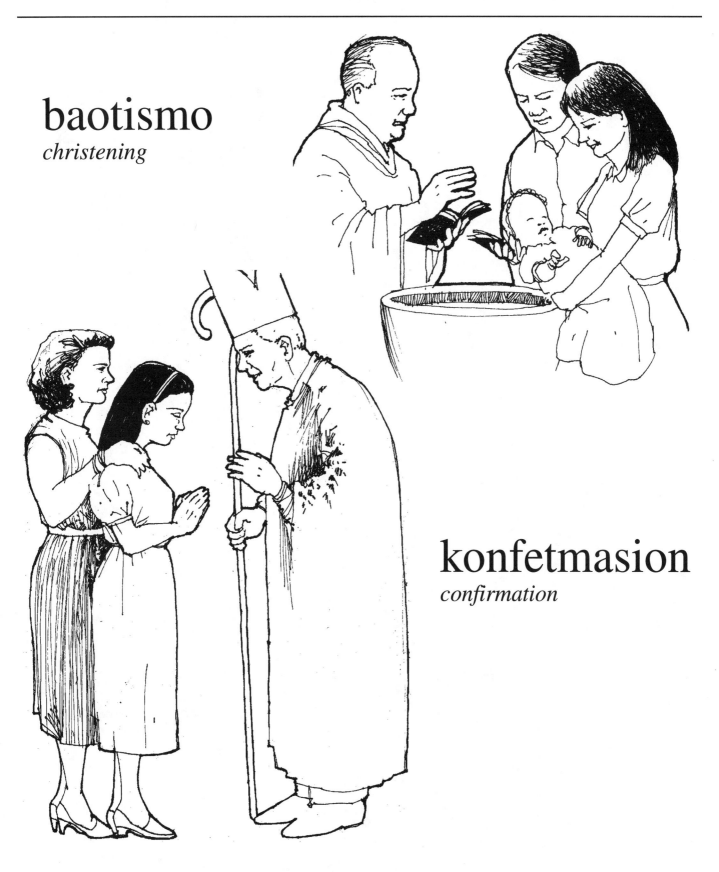

konfetmasion
confirmation

silibrasion familia *family gatherings*

komple'åños
birthday

entieru
funeral

silibrasion familia *family gatherings*

Ha'ånen Mannå'i Gråsia
Thanksgiving

Noche Buena
Christmas

silibrasion familia *family gatherings*

umakamo'
wedding

gradu'asion
graduation

betbo
action words

påra	tunnok	kånta
maila'	baila	påtek
sigi	tuge'	falågu
fatå'chong	yunga'	hugåndo
tohge	estudiha	kasse
åsson	toktok	na'gåsgas
maigo'	tåyuyot	cho'cho'
tångges	kuentos	bålle
achetge	ekungok	ta'yok
chålek	nangu	nå'i

betbo *action words*

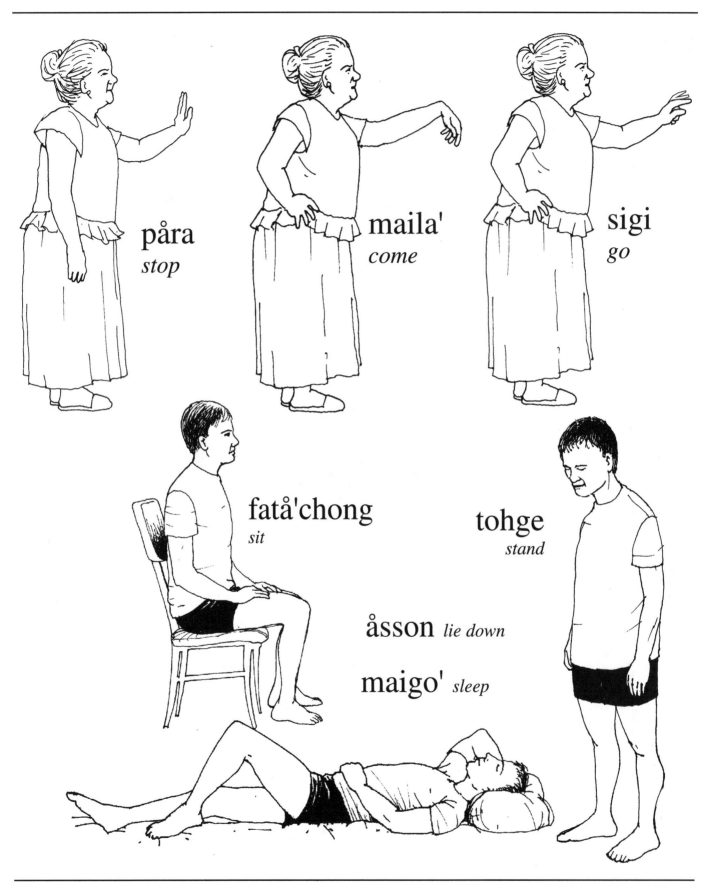

påra
stop

maila'
come

sigi
go

fatå'chong
sit

tohge
stand

åsson *lie down*

maigo' *sleep*

betbo *action words*

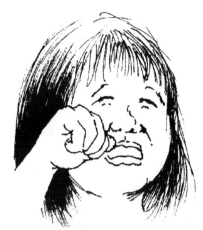

tångges *cry*

achetge *wink*

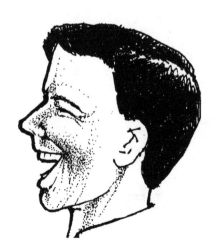

chålek *laugh*

tunnok
get down

baila
dance

tuge'
write

yunga'
draw

estudiha
study

betbo *action words*

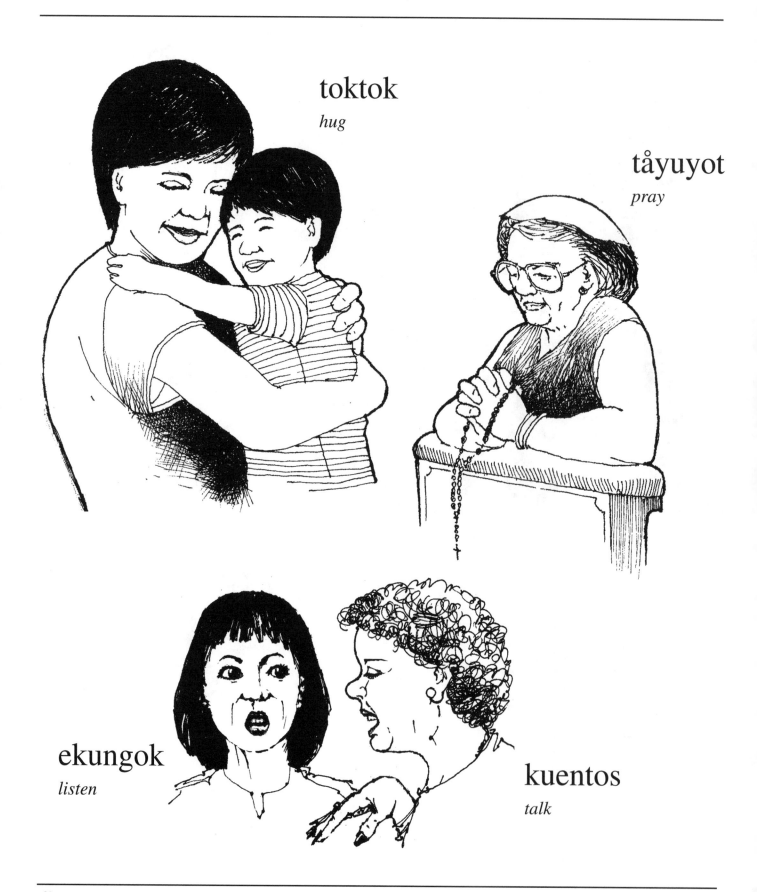

toktok
hug

tåyuyot
pray

ekungok
listen

kuentos
talk

betbo *action words*

nangu
swim

kånta
sing

påtek
kick

falågu
run

betbo *action words*

hugåndo
play

kasse
tease

na'gåsgas
clean

cho'cho'
work

bålle
sweep

ta'yok
jump

nå'i
give

chule'
take

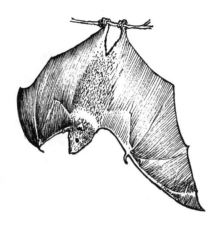

gå'ga'
animals

katu	ga'lågu	lålo'
sisata/abeha	pånglao	halu'hu
paluma	ñåmu	binådu
månnok	guali'ek	chiba
gåyu	hilitai	kabåyu
punidera	kulepbla	ko'ko'
ababang	babui	haggan
ngånga'	karabao	guihan
fanihi	akalehha'	

gå'ga' *animals*

sisata/abeha
bee

paluma
bird

katu
cat

månnok
chicken

ababang
butterfly

punidera
hen

gåyu
rooster

gå'ga' *animals*

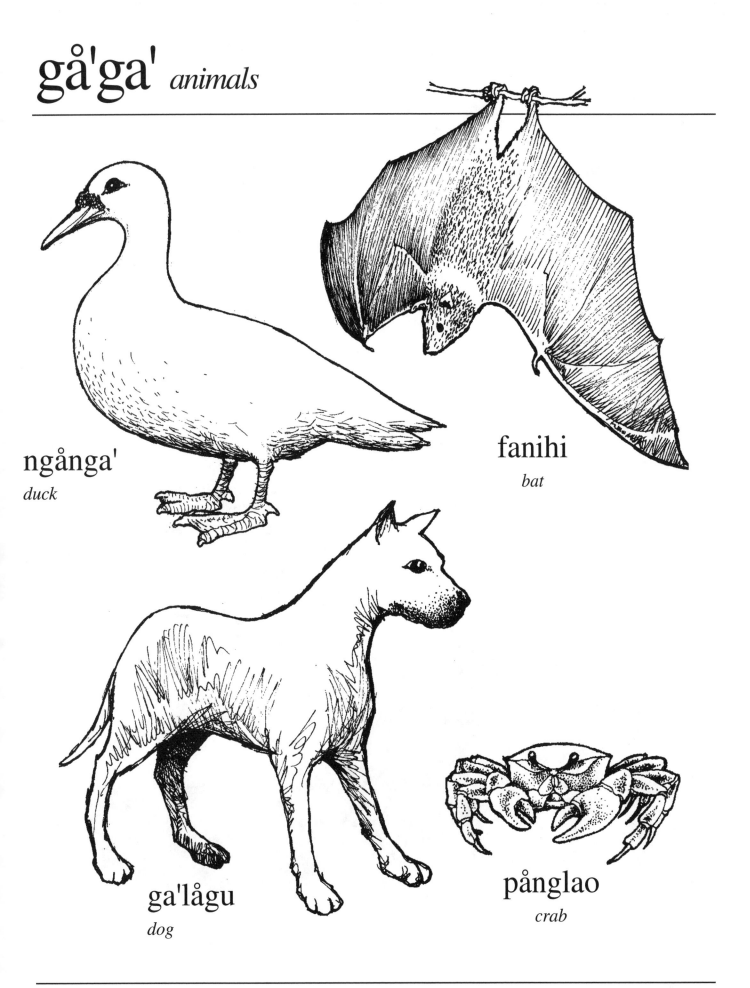

ngånga'
duck

fanihi
bat

ga'lågu
dog

pånglao
crab

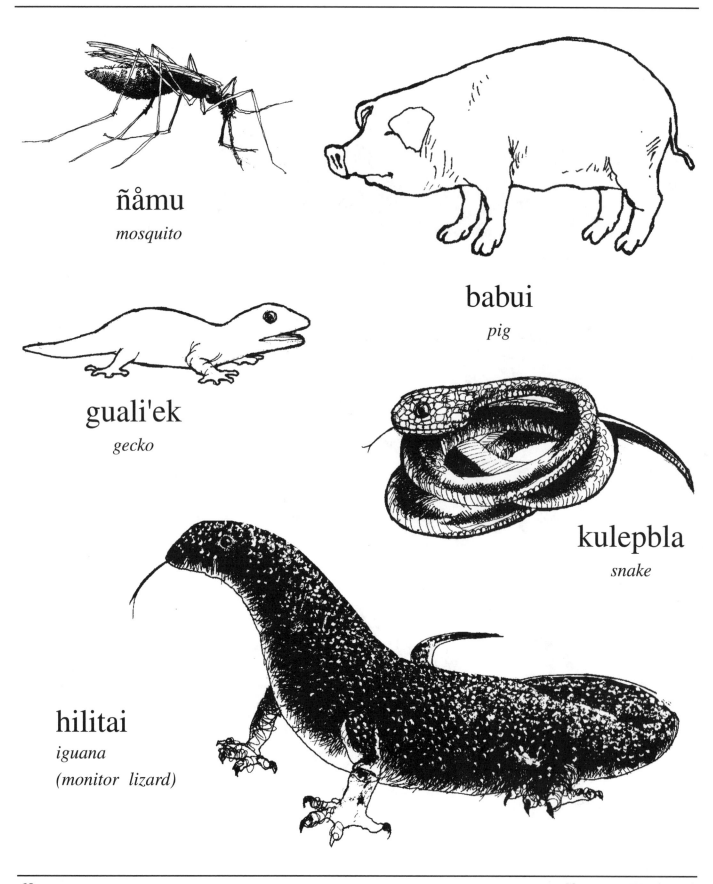

ñåmu
mosquito

babui
pig

guali'ek
gecko

kulepbla
snake

hilitai
iguana
(monitor lizard)

gå'ga' *animals*

karabao
carabao (water buffalo)

akalehha'
snail

lålo'
fly

halu'hu
shark

gå'ga' *animals*

chiba
goat

binådu
deer

kabåyu
horse

ko'ko'
Guam rail

haggan
turtle

guihan
fish

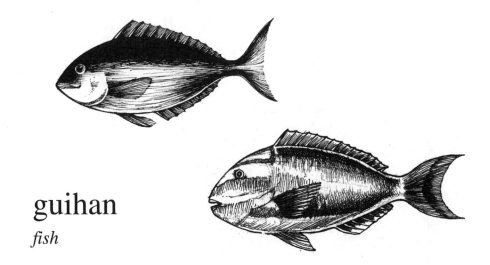

transpottasion

transportation

båtkon aire	båtko	mutusaikot
bås	boti	bisikleta
kareta/atumo-	galaide'	karetan
bet	tråk	karabao

transpottasion *transportation*

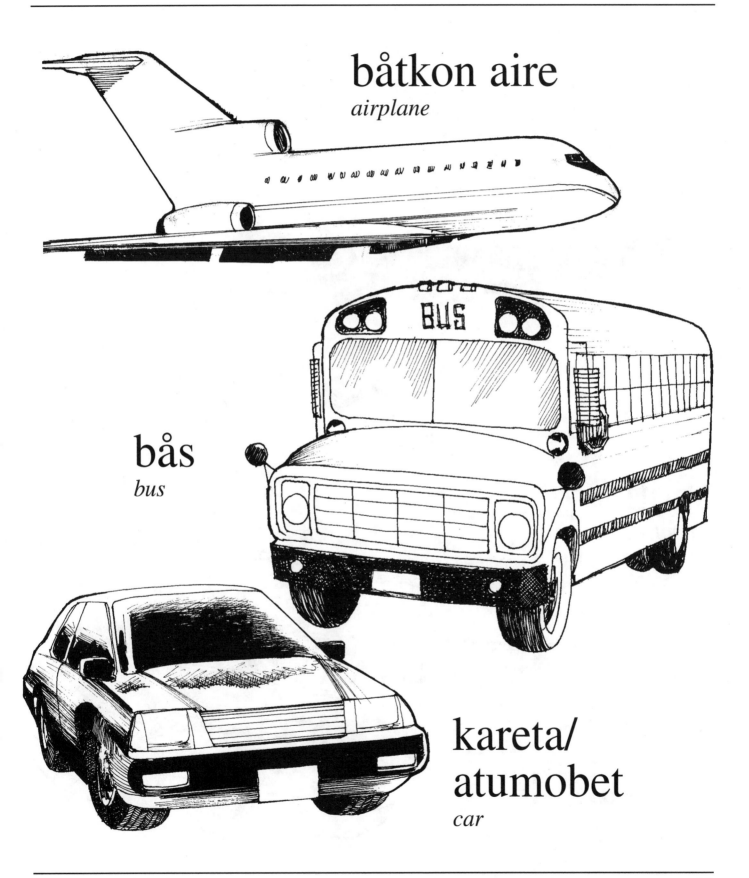

båtkon aire
airplane

bås
bus

**kareta/
atumobet**
car

transpottasion *transportation*

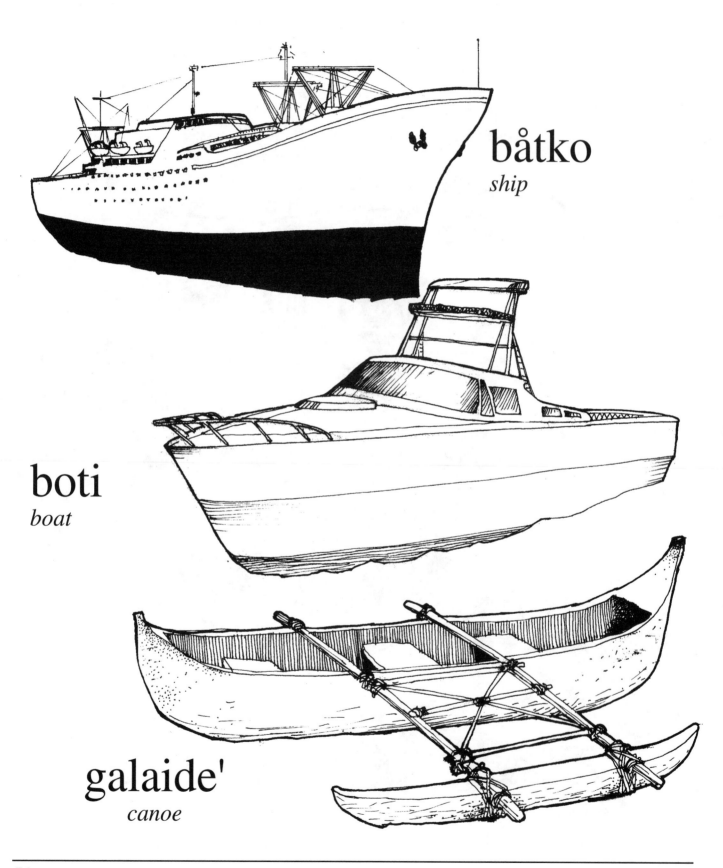

båtko
ship

boti
boat

galaide'
canoe

transpottasion *transportation*

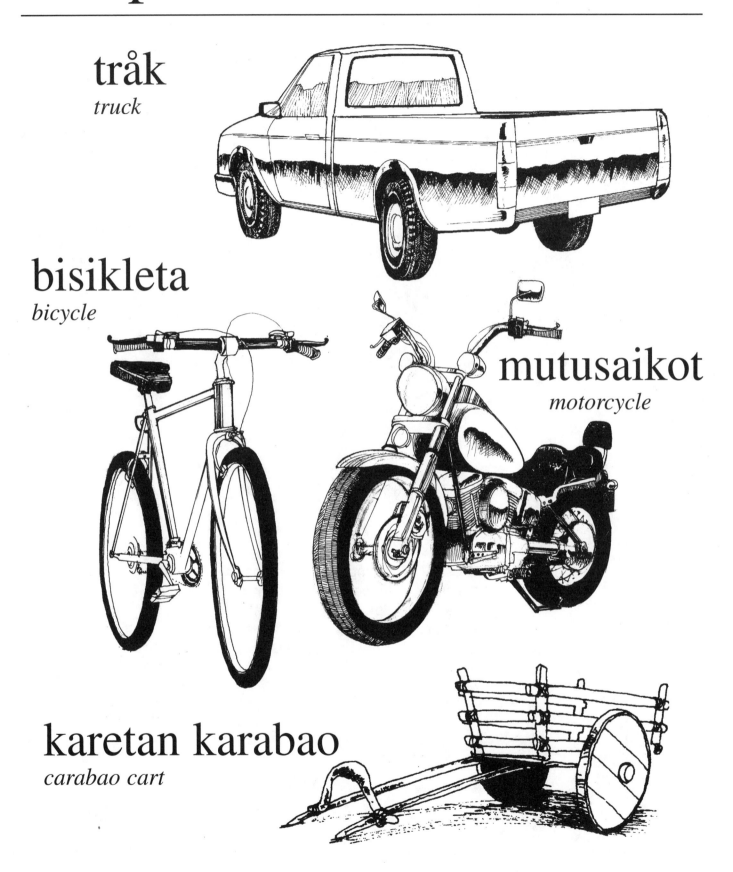

tråk
truck

bisikleta
bicycle

mutusaikot
motorcycle

karetan karabao
carabao cart

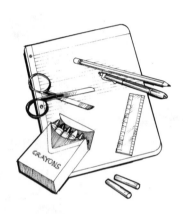

eskuela
school

ma'estra/	påppet	tiheras
ma'estro	låpes	lepblo
pisåra	pluma	litråtu
estodiånte	midida	lamasa
pålao'an	seyu	siya
låhi	kri'on	

eskuela *school*

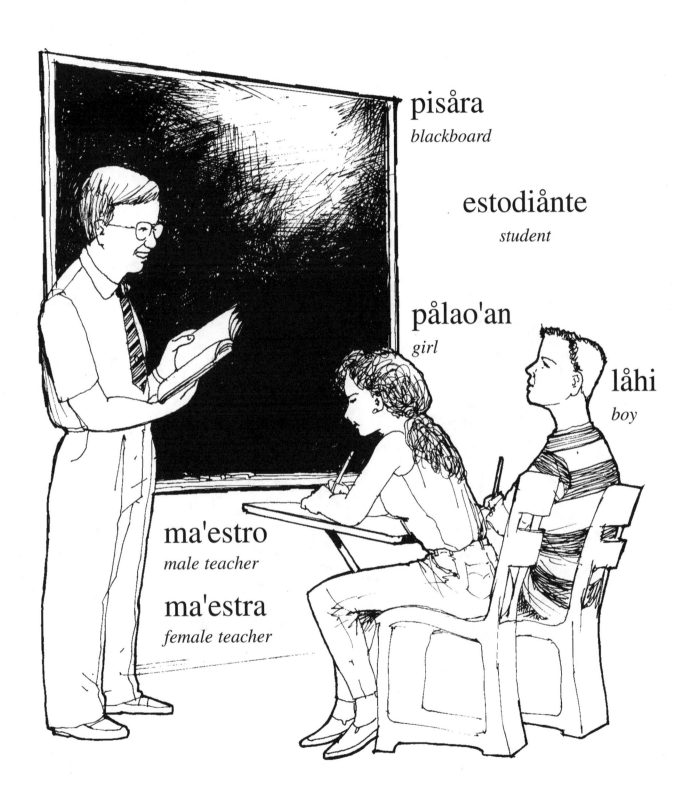

pisåra
blackboard

estodiånte
student

pålao'an
girl

låhi
boy

ma'estro
male teacher

ma'estra
female teacher

eskuela *school*

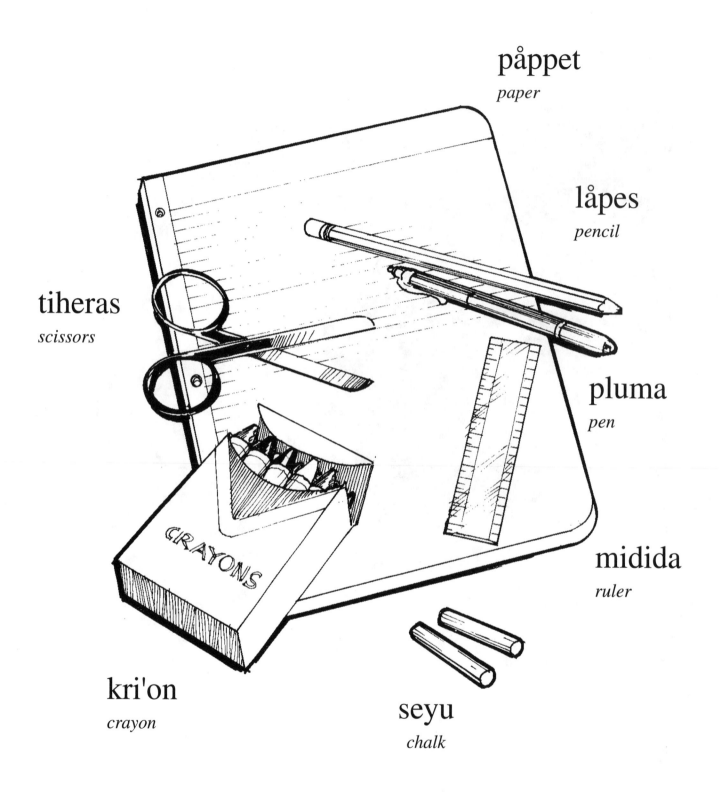

påppet
paper

låpes
pencil

tiheras
scissors

pluma
pen

midida
ruler

kri'on
crayon

seyu
chalk

eskuela *school*

lepblo
book

litråtu
picture

lamasa
desk

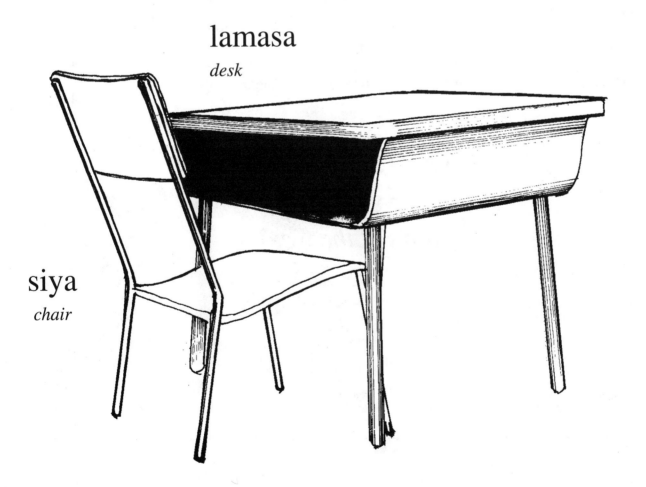

siya
chair

meses siha gi sakkan
months of the year

Ineru	Måyu	Septembre
Fibreru	Hunio	Oktubri
Måtso	Hulio	Nubembre
Abrit	Agosto	Disembre

ha'ani siha gi simana
days of the week

Damenggo	Metkoles	Betnes
Lunes	Huebes	Såbalu
Måttes		

Meses Siha Gi Sakkan
Months of the Year

Ineru *January*

Fibreru *February*

Måtso *March*

Abrit *April*

Måyu *May*

Hunio *June*

Hulio *July*

Agosto *August*

Septembre *September*

Oktubri *October*

Nubembre *November*

Disembre *December*

Ha'åni Siha Gi Simana
Days of the Week

Damenggo
Sunday

Lunes
Monday

Måttes
Tuesday

Metkoles
Wednesday

Huebes
Thursday

Betnes
Friday

Såbalu
Saturday

Nubembre *November*

Disembre *December*

Damenggo	Lunes	Måttes	Metkoles	Huebes	Betnes	Sabalu
1	2	3	4	5	6	7
8	9	10	11	12	13	14
15	16	17	18	19	20	21
22	23	24	25	26	27	28
29	30	31				

numiru siha
numbers

unu	onse	trenta
dos	dosse	kuarenta
tres	tresse	singkuenta
kuåtro	katotse	sisenta
singko	kinse	sitenta
sais	dies i sais	ochenta
siette	dies i siette	nubenta
ocho	dies i ocho	siento
nuebi	dies i nuebi	kiñentos
dies	bente	mit

numiru siha *numbers*

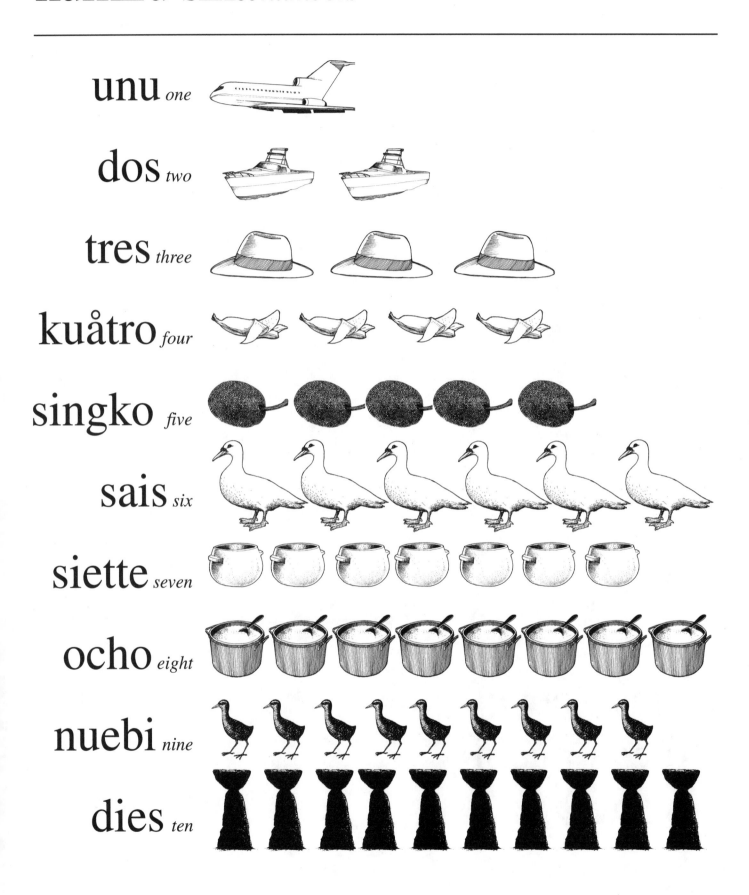

unu *one*

dos *two*

tres *three*

kuåtro *four*

singko *five*

sais *six*

siette *seven*

ocho *eight*

nuebi *nine*

dies *ten*

numiru siha *numbers*

onse *eleven*

dosse *twelve*

tresse *thirteen*

katotse *fourteen*

kinse *fifteen*

dies i sais *sixteen*

dies i siette *seventeen*

dies i ocho *eighteen*

dies i nuebi *nineteen*

bente *twenty*

trenta *thirty*

kuarenta *forty*

singkuenta *fifty*

sisenta *sixty*

sitenta *seventy*

ochenta *eighty*

nubenta *ninety*

siento *one hundred*

kiñentos *five hundred*

mit *thousand*

tiempon ha'åni

time of day

tåftaf gi	ogga'an	despues
egga'an	pupuengi	sigundo
chatangmak	talo'åni	miñutu
puengi	atrasao	ora
nigap	tåftaf	
agupa'	på'go	

tiempon ha'åni *time of day*

tåftaf gi egga'an
early morning

chatangmak
dawn

puengi
night

nigap
yesterday

agupa'
tomorrow

ogga'an
morning

pupuengi
late afternoon

talo'åni
noon

tiempon ha'åni *time of day*

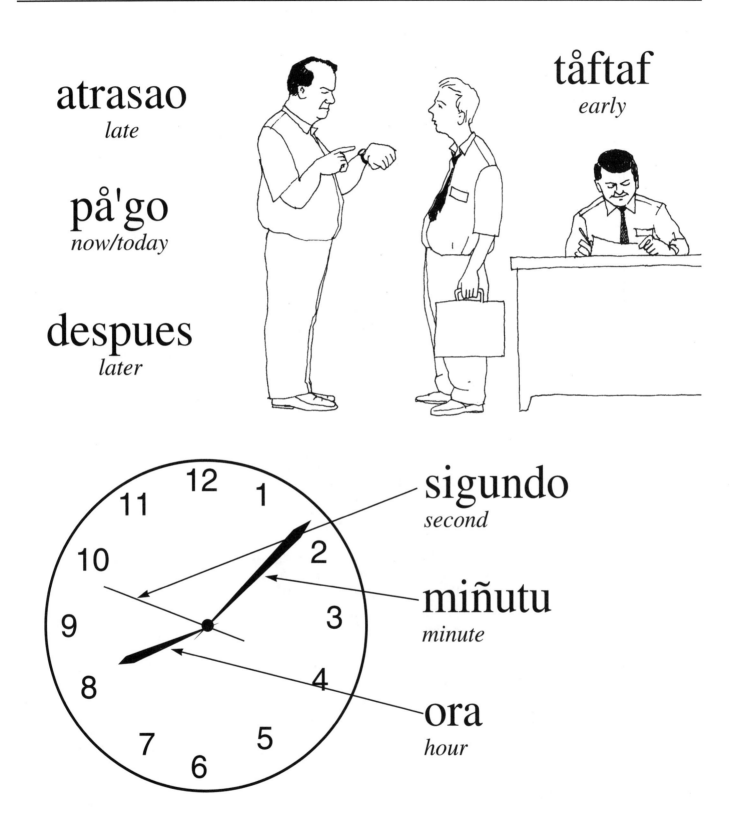

atrasao
late

tåftaf
early

på'go
now/today

despues
later

sigundo
second

miñutu
minute

ora
hour

lugåt

location

sanhalom	uriya	agapa'
sanhiyong	sanme´na	lågu
hulo'	tåtte	håya
påpa'	entalo'	kattan
sanhilo'	aka'gue	luchan
sanpapa'		

lugåt *location*

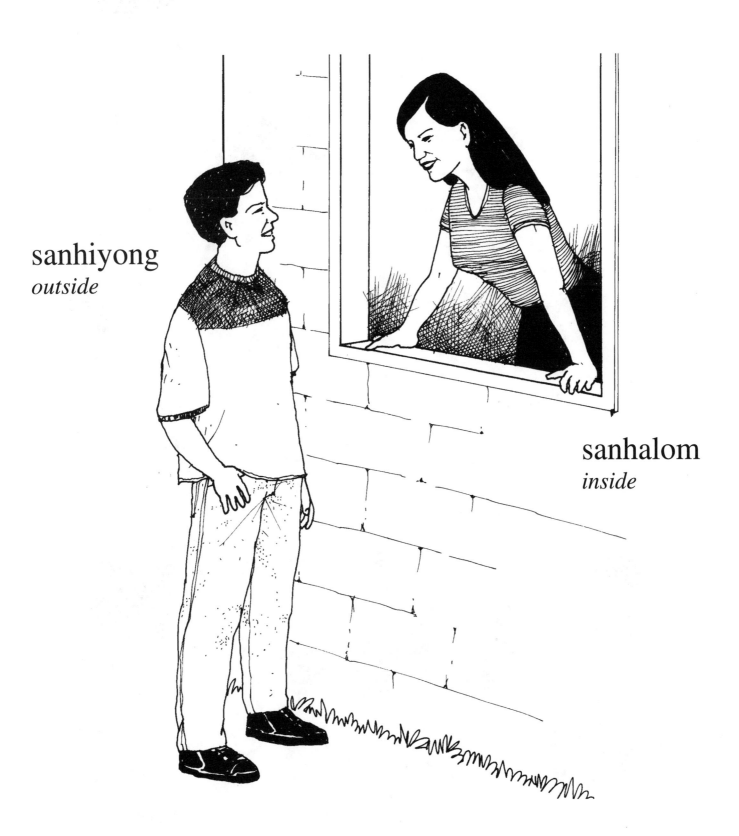

sanhiyong
outside

sanhalom
inside

lugåt *location*

sanhilo'
above or over

hulo'
up

påpa'
down

uriya *around*

lugåt *location*

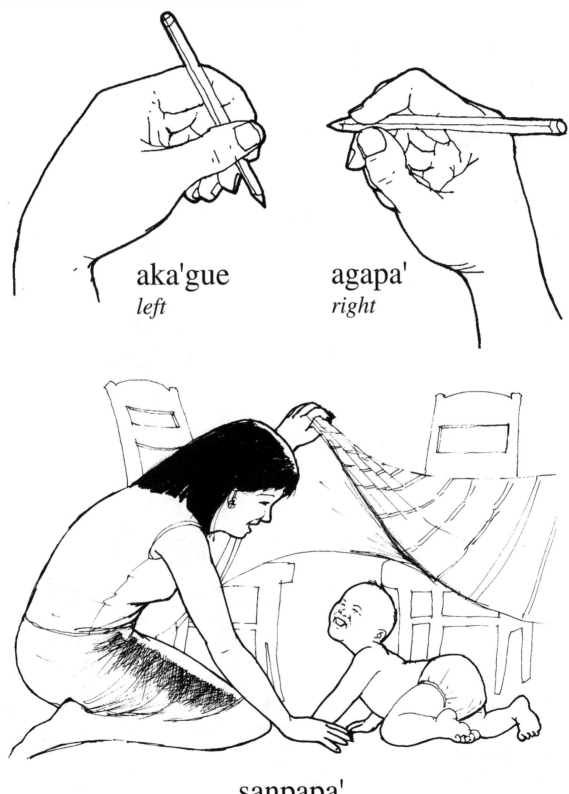

aka'gue
left

agapa'
right

sanpapa'
below or under

lugåt *location*

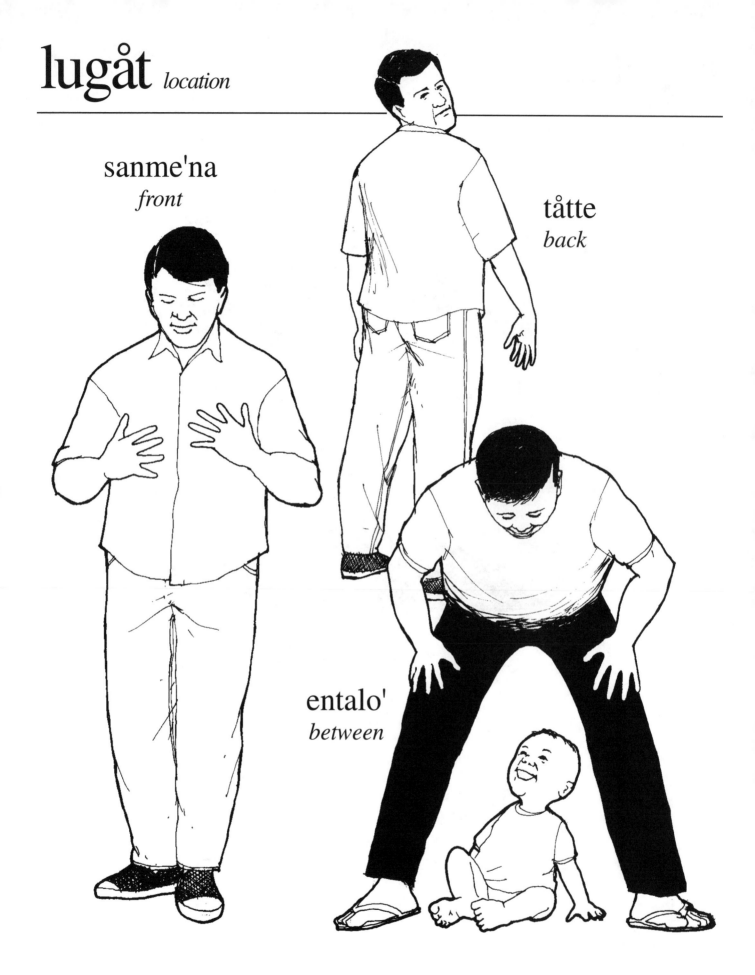

sanme'na
front

tåtte
back

entalo'
between

lugåt *location*

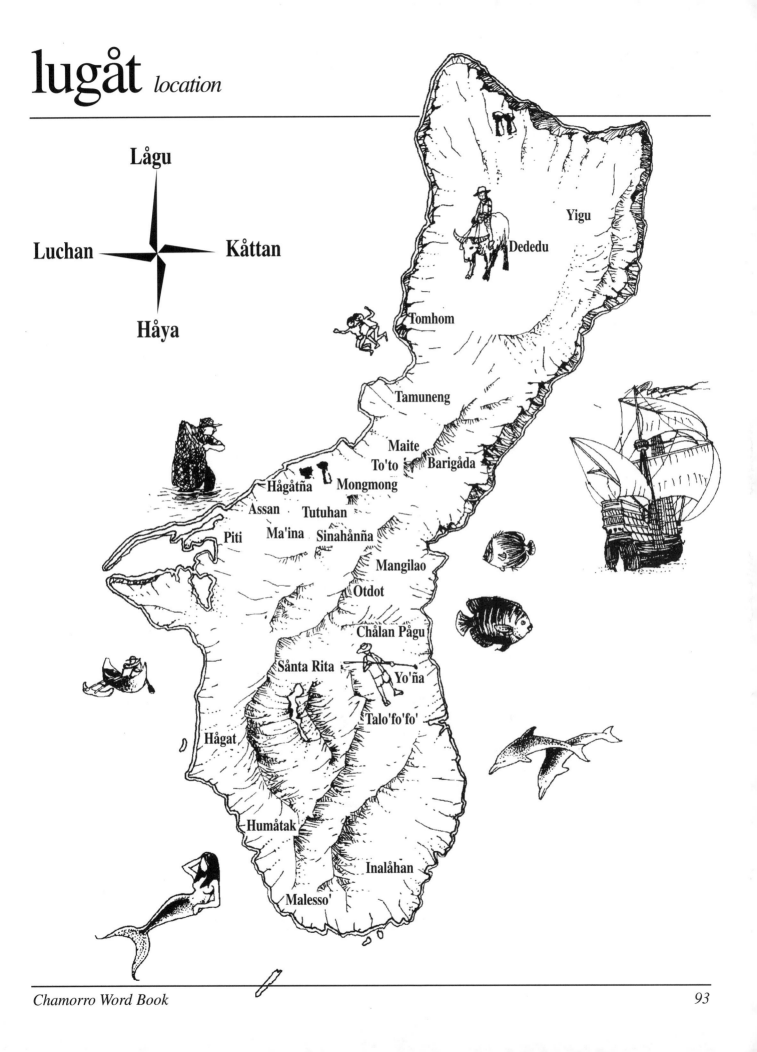

Lågu

Luchan — **Kåttan**

Håya

Yigu

Dededu

Tomhom

Tamuneng

Maite

To'to · Barigåda

Hågåtña · Mongmong

Assan · Tutuhan

Ma'ina · Sinahånña

Piti

Mangilao

Otdot

Chålan Pågu

Sånta Rita · Yo'ña

Talo'fo'fo'

Hågat

Humåtak

Inalåhan

Malesso'

kulot
colors

agaga'	asut	kulot di rosa
amariyu	lila	åttelong
kulot kåhet	kulot chukulåti	å'paka'
betde	kulot oru	kulot åpu

kulot *colors*

kulot kåhet
orange

betde
green

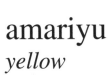

amariyu
yellow

agaga'
red

asut
blue

kulot chukulåti
brown

kulot oru
gold

kulot di rosa
pink

kulot åpu
gray

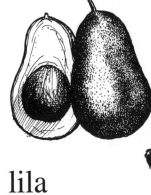

lila
purple

å'paka'
white

åttelong
black

Glossaries

Chamorro-English

ababang-butterfly
abeha-bee
Abrit-April
achetge-wink
adahi-care
adamelong-oval
aga'-ripe banana
agaga'-red
agapa'-right
agå'ga'-neck
Agosto-August
agradesi-appreciate
agupa'-tomorrow
aka'gue-left
akalehha'-snail
alageta-avocado
amariyu-yellow
amåpble-kind
anåkko'-long
anonas-custard apple
apåga-shoulder
apigige'-young coconut
   (grilled) with starch
aridondo-round
asut-blue
atrasao-late
atulen ilotes-corn soup
atumobet-car
atungo'-friends
atupat-sling
ayuda-help (verb)

å'paka'-white
åbas-guava
åchai-chin
åcho' atupat-slingstone
åddeng-foot

åhu-young coconut dessert
åmot-medicine
Åñu Nuebu-New Year
åsson-lie down
åtdao-sun
åtes-sweet sop
åttadok-eye
åttelong-black

babui-pig
baila-dance
baotismo-christening
bayogu-ankle
bålle-sweep
bås-bus
båtko-ship
båtkon aire-airplane
bente-twenty
bestidu-dress
betde-green
Betnes-Friday
bilembines-star apple
binådu-deer
bisikleta-bicycle
boti-boat
brohas-sponge cake
buñelos aga'-banana doughnuts

chachaga'-thigh
chalakiles-rice porridge
chandiha-watermelon
changkletas-slippers
chatangmak-dawn
chå-tea
chålek-laugh
chiba-goat

chigo' fruta-fruit juice
chinchule'-gift-giving
   (happy occasions)
chinina-shirt
cho'cho'-work
chotda-green banana
chule'-take

dalalai-skinny
Damenggo-Sunday
dågon håya-yam
dåma'gas-thumb
dångkolo-large
dedeggo-heel
despues-later
diamånte-diamond
dies-ten
dies i nuebi-nineteen
dies i ocho-eighteen
dies i sais-sixteen
dies i siette-seventeen
dikike'-small
Disembre-December
dos-two
dosse-twelve

ekungok-listen
ensalådan batåtas-potato
   salad
ensalådan gollai-vegetable
   salad
entalo'-between
entieru-funeral
eskuela-school
estodiånte-student
estreyas-star
estudiha-study

Chamorro-English

falågu-run
fanihi-bat
fatå'chong-sit
fåsu-cheek
Fibreru-February
figura siha-shapes
fina'denne'-hot sauce
franela-t-shirt

ga'lågu-dog
galaide'-canoe
gapotulu-hair
gåyu-rooster
gradu'asion-graduation
guali'ek-gecko
gui'eng-nose
guihan-fish
gupot i sengsong-village fiesta

Ha'ånen Mannå'i Gråsia-
　Thanksgiving
Ha'ånen Mannåna-
　Mother´s Day
Ha'ånen Mantåta-
　Father´s Day
Ha'ånen Sånta Maria
　Kåmalen-Our Lady of
　Camarin Day
ha'åni-day
haggan-turtle
hagon suni-taro leaf
haguet-hook
halu'hu-shark
hammon-ham
hå'i-forehead
hånom-water
håya-south
hilitai-iguana

hineksa'-rice
hinetnon babui-roast pig
hotno-oven
Huebes-Thursday
hugåndo-play
Hulio-July
hulo'-up
Hunio-June

ika- gift-giving
　(sad occasions)
ina'ayuda-help
ina'fa'maolek-getting along
ina'guaiya-love
ina'påtte-share
inadahi-care
inagofli'e'-kindness
Ineru-January

kabåyu-horse
kadada'-short
kafe-coffee
kalamai-corn pudding
kanton tåsi-shore
karabao-carabao (water buf-
　falo)
kareta-car
karetan karabao-carabao
　cart
kasse-tease
katsunes-pants
katsunes kadada'-shorts
katsunes umo'mak-swim-
　ming trunks
katotse-fourteen
katu-cat
kåddon månnok-chicken
　soup

kåhet-orange
kålulot-finger
kålulot åddeng-toe
kånnai-hand
kånta-sing
kåttan-east
kek Chamoru-Chamorro
　cake
kelaguen månnok-lemon
　chicken
kiñåda-sister-in-law
kiñådu-brother-in-law
kiñentos-five hundred
kinse-fifteen
klåsi-kind
ko'ko'-Guam rail
komple'åños-birthday
konfetmasion-confirmation
konsederasion-consideration
kostumbre-tradition
kri'on-crayon
kuadrao-square
kuarenta-forty
kuåtro-four
kuchåla-spoon
kuentos-talk
kueyu-neck (back of)
kulepbla-snake
kulot åpu-gray
kulot chukulåti-brown
kulot di rosa-pink
kulot kåhet-orange
kulot oru-gold
kusinan sanhiyong-outside
　kitchen

laguanå-sour sop
lamasa-desk

Chamorro-English

latte-stone pillar for building
låbios-lips
lågu-north
lålo'-fly
låpes-pencil
lemmai-breadfruit
lepblo-book
libra-pound
lila-purple
litråtu-picture
lokka'-tall
lommok-pestle
luchan-west
lugåt-location
Lunes-Monday
lupes-skirt
lusong-grinding bowl

ma'estra-teacher (female)
ma'estro-teacher (male)
magågon bahåki-ranch
   clothes
magågon maigo'-pajamas
magågu-clothes
maigo'-sleep
maila'-come
makkat-heavy
mandanña-getting together
mannginge'-kiss or smell
   hand
masoksok-skinny
mångga-mango
månglo'-breeze, wind
månnok-chicken
månu-pestle
måta-face
Måtso-March
Måttes-Tuesday

Måyu-May
mediu sitkolo-semicircle
melon-melon
mestisa-traditional dress
Metkoles-Wednesday
meyas-socks
midiånu-medium
midida-ruler
mineddong-sizes
miñutu-minute
mit-thousand
mitåti-corn-grinding stone
muñekan kånnai-wrist
mutusaikot-motorcycle

na'gåsgas-clean
ñalalang-light
nangu-swim
nå'i-give
ñåmu-mosquito
nåna-mother
nånan biha-grandmother
neni-baby
ngånga'-duck
nifen-teeth
nigap-yesterday
niyok-coconut
Noche Buena-Christmas
ñora-respect to elderly
   woman
ñot-respect to elderly man
Nubembre-November
nubenta-ninety
nuebi-nine

ochenta-eighty
ocho-eight
ogga'an-morning

Oktubri-October
onsa-ounce
onse-eleven
ora-hour

paluma-bird
papåya-papaya
på'go-today, now
påchot-mouth
påkyo-typhoon
pån-bread
pånglao-crab
påñu-handkerchief
påpa'-down
påppet-paper
påra-stop
Påsgua-Easter
påsu-clay pot
påtek-kick
påtgon låhi-boy (child); son
påtgon pålaoan-girl
   (child); daughter
pecho-chest
petna-leg
piña-pineapple
pineddong hånom-waterfall
pisåra-blackboard
plåtu-plate
plomu-sinker
pluma-pen
prima-cousin (female)
primu-cousin (male)
puengi-night
pugua'-betel nut
punidera-hen
pupuengi-late afternoon
pupulu-mint leaf

Chamorro-English

rektånggolo-rectangle
respetu-respect

saddok-river
sais-six
sandalihas-sandals
sanhalom-inside
sanhilo'-above, over
sanhiyong-outside
sanme'na-front
sanpapa'-below, under
saosao kånnai-napkin
sapåtos-shoes
sapåtos goma-tennis shoes
Såbalu-Saturday
sehas-eyebrow
sentoron-belt
Septembre-September
seyu-chalk
siento-one hundred
siette-seven
sigi-go
sigundo-second
Simåna Sånta-Holy Week
singko-five
singkuenta-fifty
sisata-bee
sisenta-sixty
sitenta-seventy
siya-chair
somnak-sunshine
subrina-niece

subrinu-nephew
suni-taro

ta'yok-jump
talanga-ear
talo'åni-noon
tåftaf-early
tåftaf gi egga'an-early morning
tåhgong-shell
tångges-cry
tåsi-ocean
tåta-father
tåtalo'-back
tåtan bihu-grandfather
tåtaotao-body
tåtte-back
tåyuyot-pray
tenidot-fork
tiha-auntie
tiheras-scissors
tihu-uncle
tinahlang-weight
tingteng-waterfall
tininon kosteyas-barbecued spareribs
titiyas-tortillas
tohge-stand
tokcha'-fishing spear
toktok-hug
tommo-knee
tommon kånnai-elbow

tongho-neck (back of)
tradision-tradition
transpottasion-transportation
tråhen numangu-bathing suit
tråk-truck
trenta-thirty
tres-three
tresse-thirteen
triånggolo-triangle
trongkon kånnai-arm
trongkon niyok-coconut tree
tuge'-write
tuhong-hat
tunilåda-ton
tunnok-get down
tuyan-stomach

uchan-rain
uhang-shrimp
ulu-head
umakamo'-wedding
unai-sand
unu-one
uriya-around

yommok-fat
yore'-slippers
yunga'-draw

English - Chamorro

above-sanhilo'
airplane-båtkon aire
ankle-bayogu
appreciate-agradesi
April-Abrit
arm-trongkon kånnai
around-uriya
August-Agosto
auntie-tiha
avocado-alageta

baby-neni
back (adverb)-tåtte
back (body part)-tåtalo'
banana (green)-chotda
banana (ripe)-aga'
banana doughnuts-buñelos
    aga'
barbecued spareribs-tininon
    kosteyas
bat-fanihi
bathing suit-tråhen numangu
bee-sisata, abeha
below-sanpapa'
belt-sentoron
betel nut-pugua'
between-entalo'
bicycle-bisikleta
bird-paluma
birthday-komple'åños
black-åttelong
blackboard-pisåra
blue-asut
boat-boti
body-tåtaotao
book-lepblo

boy-påtgon låhi
bread-pån
breadfruit-lemmai
breeze-månglo'
brother-in-law-kiñådu
brown-kulot chukulåti
bus-bås
butterfly-ababang

canoe-galaide'
car-kareta/atumobet
carabao (water buffalo)-
    karabao
carabao cart-karetan
    karabao
care-adahi/inadahi
cat-katu
chair-siya
chalk-seyu
Chamorro cake-kek
    Chamoru
cheek-fåsu
chest-pecho
chicken-månnok
chicken soup-kåddon mån-
    nok
chin-åchai
christening-baotismo
Christmas-Noche Buena
clay pot-påsu
clean-na'gåsgas
clothes-magågu
coconut-niyok
coconut tree-trongkon niyok
coffee-kafe
come-maila'

confirmation-konfetmasion
consideration-konsederasion
corn-grinding stone-mitåti
corn pudding-kalamai
corn soup-atulen ilotes
cousin (male)-primu
cousin (female)-prima
crab-pånglao
crayon-kri'on
cry-tångges
custard apple-anonas

dance-baila
daughter-påtgon pålao'an
dawn-chatangmak
day-ha'åni
December-Disembre
deer-binådu
desk-lamasa
diamond-diamånte
dog-ga'lågu
down-påpa'
draw-yunga'
dress-bestidu
dress (traditional)-mestisa
duck-ngånga'

ear-talanga
early-tåftaf
early morning-tåftaf gi
    egga'an
east-kåttan
Easter-Påsgua
eight-ocho
eighteen-dies i ocho
eighty-ochenta

elbow-tommon kånnai
eleven-onse
eye-åttadok
eyebrow-sehas

face-måta
fat-yommok
father-tåta
Father's Day-Ha'ånen
    Mantåta
February-Fibreru
fifteen-kinse
fifty-singkuenta
finger-kålulot
fish-guihan
fishing spear-tokcha'
five-singko
five hundred-kiñentos
fly-lålo'
foot-åddeng
forehead-hå'i
fork-tenidot
forty-kuarenta
four-kuåtro
fourteen-katotse
Friday-Betnes
friends-atungo'
front-sanme'na
fruit juice-chigo' fruta
funeral-entieru

gecko-guali'ek
get down-tunnok
getting along-ina'fa'maolek
getting together-mandañña'
gift-giving (happy occasions-
    chinchule'

gift-giving (sad occasions)
    ika
girl-påtgon pålao'an
give-nå'i
go-sigi
goat-chiba
gold-kulot oru
graduation-gradu'asion
grandfather-tåtan bihu
grandmother-nånan biha
gray-kulot åpu
green-betde
green banana-chotda
grinding bowl-lusong
grinding stone-mitåti
Guam rail-ko'ko'
guava-åbas

hair-gapotulu
ham-hammon
hand-kånnai
handkerchief-påñu
hat-tuhong
head-ulu
healer-suruhånu
heavy-makkat
heel-dedeggo
help (noun)-ina'ayuda
help (verb)-ayuda
hen-punidera
Holy Week-Simåna Sånta
hook-haguet
horse-kabåyu
hot sauce-fina'denne'
hour-ora
hug-toktok
hundred-siento

iguana-hilitai
inside-sanhalom

January-Ineru
July-Hulio
jump-ta'yok
June-Hunio

kick-påtek
kind-amåpble, klåsi
kindness-inagofli'e'
kiss or smell hand-
    manninge'
knee-tommo

large-dångkolo
late-atrasao
late afternoon-pupuengi
later-despues
laugh-chålek
left-aka'gue
leg-petna
lemon chicken- kelaguen
    månnok
lie down-åsson
light-ñalalang
lips-låbios
listen-ekungok
location-lugåt
long-anåkko'
love-ina'guaiya

mango-mångga
March-Måtso
May-Måyu
medicine-åmot
medium-midiånu

English - Chamorro

melon-melon
mint leaf-pupulu
minute-miñutu
Monday-Lunes
monitor lizard-hilitai
morning-ogga'an
mortar-mitåti
mosquito-ñåmu
mother-nåna
Mother's Day-Ha'ånen
   Mannåna
motorcycle-mutusaikot
mouth-påchot

napkin-saosao kånnai
neck-agå'ga'
neck (back of)-tongho,
   kueyu
nephew-subrinu
New Year-Añu Nuebu
niece-subrina
night-puengi
nine-nuebi
nineteen-dies i nuebi
ninety-nubenta
noon-talo'åni
north-lågu
nose-gui'eng
November-Nubembre
now-på'go

ocean-tåsi
October-Oktubri
one-unu
one hundred-siento
orange (color)-kulot kåhet
orange (fruit)-kåhet

ounce-onsa
Our Lady of Camarin Day-
   Ha'ånen Sånta Maria
   Kåmalen
outside-sanhiyong
outside kitchen-kusinan sanhiyong
oval-adamelong
oven-hotno
over-sanhilo'

pajamas-magågon maigo'
pants-katsunes
papaya-papåya
paper-påppet
pen-pluma
pencil-låpes
pestle-lommok, månu
picture-litråtu
pig-babui
pineapple-piña
pink-kulot di rosa
plate-plåtu
play-hugåndo
potato salad-ensalådan batå-
   tas
pound-libra
pray-tåyuyot
purple-lila

rain-uchan
ranch clothes-magågon
   bahåki
rectangle-rektånggolo
red-agaga'
respect-respetu
respect to elderly man-ñot

respect to elderly woman-
   ñora
rice-hineksa'
rice porridge-chalakiles
right-agapa'
river-saddok
roast pig-hinetnon babui
rooster-gåyu
round-aridondo
ruler-midida
run-falågu

sand-unai
sandals-sandalihas
Saturday-Såbalu
school-eskuela
scissors-tiheras
second-sigundo
semicircle-mediu sitkolo
September-Septembre
seven-siette
seventeen-dies i siette
seventy-sitenta
shapes-figura siha
share-ina'påtte
shark-halu'hu
shell-tåhgong
ship-båtko
shirt-chinina
shoes-sapåtos
shore-kanton tåsi
short-kadada'
shorts-katsunes kadada'
shoulder-apåga
shrimp-uhang
sing-kånta
sinker-plomu

sister-in-law-kiñåda
sit-fatå'chong
six-sais
sixteen-dies i sais
sixty-sisenta
sizes-mineddong
skinny-dalalai, masoksok
skirt-lupes
sleep-maigo'
sling-atupat
slingstone-åcho' atupat
slippers-chankletas, yore
small-dikike'
smile-chatge
snail-akalehha'
snake-kulepbla
socks-meyas
son-påtgon låhi
sour sop-laguanå
south-håya
sponge cake-brohas
spoon-kuchåla
square-kuadrao
stand-tohge
star-estreyas
star apple-bilembines
stomach-tuyan
stone pillar for building-latte
stop-påra
student-estodiånte
study-estudiha
sun-åtdao
Sunday-Damenggo
sunshine-somnak
sweep-bålle
sweet sop-åtes
swim-nangu

swimming trunks-katsunes umo'mak

take-chule'
talk-kuentos
tall-lokka'
tapioca-mende'oka
taro-suni
taro leaf-hagon suni
tea-chå
teacher (female)-ma'estra
teacher (male) -ma'estro
tease-kasse
teeth-nifen
ten-dies
tennis shoes-sapåtos goma
Thanksgiving-Ha'ånen Mannå'i Gråsia
thigh-chachaga'
thirteen-tresse
thirty-trenta
thousand-mit
three-tres
thumb-dåma'gas
Thursday-Huebes
today-pa'go
toe-kålulot åddeng
tomorrow-agupa'
ton-tunilåda
tortillas-titiyas
tradition-kostumbre, tradision
traditional dress-mestisa
transportation-transpottasion
triangle-triånggolo
truck-tråk
t-shirt-franela

Tuesday-Måttes
turtle-haggan
twelve-dosse
twenty-bente
two-dos
typhoon-påkyo

uncle-tihu
under-sanpapa
up-hulo'

vegetable salad-ensalådan gollai
village fiesta-gupot i seng song

water-hånom
water buffalo (carabao)-karabao
waterfall-tingteng (peneddong hånom)
watermelon-chandiha
wedding-umakamo'
Wednesday-Metkoles
weight-tinahlang
west-luchan
white-å'paka'
wind-månglo'
wink-achetge
work-cho'cho'
wrist-muñekan kånnai
write-tuge'

yam-dågon håya
yellow-amariyu
yesterday-nigap
young coconut dessert-åhu
young coconut (grilled) with starch-apigige'

If you enjoyed the *Chamorro Word Book*, look for these other books about GUAM from The Bess Press:

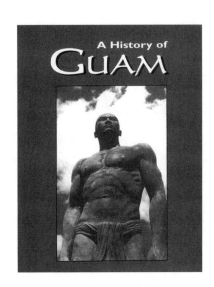
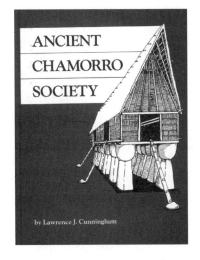